MeToo

Dedicated to Jayalakshmi Venugopal, a feminist in times and spaces where it wasn't always easy, and the best mother anyone could have.

MeToo

The Impact of Rape Culture in the Media

Meenakshi Gigi Durham

polity

First published in 2021 by Polity Press

Polity Press
65 Bridge Street
Cambridge CB2 1UR, UK

Polity Press
101 Station Landing
Suite 300
Medford, MA 02155, USA

ISBN-13: 978-1-5095-3519-4
ISBN-13: 978-1-5095-3520-0 (pb)

A catalogue record for this book is available from the British Library.

Typeset in 11 on 14 Sabon
by Fakenham Prepress Solutions, Fakenham, Norfolk NR21 8NL
Printed and bound in the UK by TJ Books Limited

For further information on Polity, visit our website:
politybooks.com

Contents

Contents

Acknowledgments

This book came to its conclusion in turbulent times, as a deadly virus wracked the globe and Black Lives Matter demonstrations called out the ongoing crisis of racial injustice. Writing was challenging, in part because of the emotional toll these events took, and in part because I couldn't easily get to the library or to my office at the University of Iowa. So I wrote at home, in between checking news feeds, and I am eternally grateful to my family for understanding and support, as random stacks of books piled up everywhere and I huddled with my laptop behind closed doors. My heartfelt thanks go to my husband Frank, who (as he has done for years) mulled over ideas with me, read and edited draft chapters, brought me cups of coffee when my energy was flagging, and got me to take exercise breaks. My daughters Sonali and Maya inspire me every day with their commitment to feminism and racial and social justice. I'm also deeply grateful to the University of Iowa librarians, especially Tim Arnold and Donald Baxter, for helping me obtain the materials I needed even when campus was officially closed. The amazing colleagues and friends who have supported and encouraged me have my deepest gratitude: I feel lucky to be part of such a lively and collaborative community. Many thanks to Mary Savigar and Ellen MacDonald-Kramer at Polity Books for believing in this project and for their encouragement, knowledge, and patience.

Most of all I thank my mother, Jayalakshmi Venugopal, for her brilliance, sense of humor, and love. Her passing this year has left a chasm in the world.

In ancient Greece, Pandora's box was not actually a box but a jar, or a clay pot with a lid that was kept in the kitchen, where the women were also kept. Maybe it contained evil—or maybe it just concealed it. Maybe Pandora let the evil out, or maybe she blew the lid off what was really going on back there, where nobody else could see it. Anyway, the truth got out, and all hell broke loose, leaving behind only hope.

Carina Chocano, "Plain Sight," *New York Times Magazine*, November 26, 2017, p. 13

A feminist ear can be how you hear what is not being heard.

Sara Ahmed, *Living a Feminist Life*, 2016, p. 203.

Introduction

The media are a linchpin in the contemporary feminist movement against sexual violence.

We are in a "MeToo[1] moment"—or so the media tell us. The very term is a media goldmine: not only is it jauntily alliterative, but it seems to have an instantly recognizable meaning. It pops up in headlines and in TV news teasers whenever a famous man is accused of sexual abuse, assault, or harassment, which seems to happen on the hour somewhere in the world.

Although sexual misconduct in the workplace and elsewhere is not a new issue and feminist activism against sex assault has persevered for at least a century now, the intensity of the global upheavals of this MeToo moment marks a striking social shift. The scope and virality of MeToo/#MeToo have exceeded those of any previous online organizing effort around sexual violence.[2] The movement is variously referred to as a "culture shock," a "tsunami," or an "explosion," since its ripple effects are being experienced in life-changing ways at multiple levels across the world.

The media are in fact, quite literally, sites of sexual violence: for decades, sexual harassment and assault have been routinized and concealed in corporate media workplaces. Acts of rape have been committed in newsrooms, on film sets, in media executives' hotel rooms. The strategies used by many media corporations to conceal, and thereby enable, serial sexual assaults show that sexual violence is systemic violence, embedded in the structures of workplaces and buttressed by other institutional mechanisms, such as legal processes and human resources (HR) policies. In the wake of #MeToo, it has become increasingly apparent that these mechanisms and structures are deeply entrenched in a variety of social institutions and in most countries and cultures. The media industries are not unique, but they have awakened a realization that workplaces harbor a rape culture—a culture that not only facilitates rape but, perhaps most damningly, silences its survivors. Media worksites, mediated images and messages, and media social networks all serve to illuminate the way sexual violence percolates throughout societies. The media's relationship with rape culture is thus of vital contemporary importance.

This book centers on rape culture in the media, especially with regard to the silencing and the silence breaking of survivors of sexual violence, practices that have shaped rape culture in multiple and complex ways. This focus on silence as systemic, especially in the media, contributes new insights into our understanding of rape culture.

Silence has always haunted sexual violence. Terrorized, shamed, or discounted, survivors have had to harbor their sexual assaults as dark secrets, often coping with the trauma and the injury while they were bereft of support systems or resources. Media corporations such as Miramax and Fox News actively silenced and concealed the acts of sexual violence that occurred in their workplaces for decades. Yet the media—social media—were also key to the breaking of silence when #MeToo erupted in 2017; and the media are sites where many dimensions of rape culture have been exposed, through representation, discourse, and commentary.

Rape culture, as a concept, has become highly visible in this MeToo moment. It is a hotly contested term and idea, which refers basically to "a complex of beliefs that encourages male sexual aggression and supports violence against women," leading to the acceptance of rape as a normal part of life.[3] While this definition addresses the societal dynamics that embed rape in everyday life, it rests on a male–female gender binary that doesn't capture the diversity and range of experiences of sexual violence. Statistically, perpetrators tend to be cisgender straight men, but sometimes people of other genders initiate sexual violence too, so that rape occurs across categories of race, class, gender, nation, sexual orientation, and other intersectional categories of identity.

Recognizing this, it becomes important to construe rape culture in terms of sexual power that has been historically entrenched and culturally validated: the kind of sexual power that tacitly condones rape as an explicitly sexual expression of dominance. Nor is "rape culture" limited to any legal definition of "rape," as it encompasses a range of sexually aggressive behaviors that sustain sexual power relations and reinforce an individual's sexual violability as a result of social classification.

Critics of the concept of rape culture reject it on the premise that the "developed" societies of the global North are relatively rape-free and penalize rape severely by comparison to the societies of the global South. These claims are disputable, both because rape is vastly underreported everywhere and because penalties vary, especially when social vectors such as race, class, and citizenship status are taken into account. As the second-wave feminist scholar Susan Griffin pointed out, "[t]he fact that rape is against the law should not be considered proof that rape is not in fact encouraged as part of our culture."[4] The concept of rape culture as a framework has been validated by the #MeToo hashtag and its aftermath: the millions of tweets and social media discourses swiftly exposed the pervasiveness of sexual violence in most societies. In doing so, they engaged with rape culture in myriad ways, at once recognizing, resisting, and reevaluating the concept from multiple perspectives.

From these online engagements it has become clear that the media are not only the physical sites of rape culture in the workplace, they are also an active *discursive* site of interrogation about rape and the cultures that produce it, sustain it, and conceal it. Like Tarana Burke's "me too™" movement, #MeToo served in the first place to create a space for survivors to voice the experience of sexual violence, as it was impelled by a keen recognition that accounts of sexual abuse and assault are routinely stifled by dominant institutions and their powers of insidious sexual censorship. I use the term "censorship" to claim, not that survivors' stories are explicitly excised from any public record, but rather that sexual violence survivors face powerful cultural silencing mechanisms that often prevent them from disclosing their victimization: they are disbelieved, blamed for the assault, accused of wanting and even enjoying it, retraumatized through enforced retellings of the incident and brutal interrogations about it, persuaded to take hush money and sign nondisclosure agreements, shunned by families and communities as a consequence of their injury, stigmatized, and even persecuted or prosecuted. Hence #MeToo served a "silence-breaking" purpose, providing an outlet for speaking the realities of sexual violence in which survivors could find a community of support. Such movements had been emerging in many spaces and places around the globe; #MeToo, for a variety of reasons, including its genesis in the United States and its connections to powerful white celebrity women, both accelerated these movements and eclipsed them.

Survivors' ability to speak is inflected by race, class, gender, and other intersecting sociocultural factors. The legal scholar Angela Onwuachi-Willig has pointed out that "[t]he recent resurgence of the #MeToo movement reflects the longstanding marginalization and exclusion that women of color experience within the larger feminist movement in US society,"[5] despite the fact that women of color have been in the vanguard of legal action and community organizing against sexual violence, and despite their greater vulnerability to both sexual harassment and silencing.

In all these ways, the so-called MeToo moment,

itself a media invention, highlights the implications of rape culture for our media organizations, representations, and discourses. That, as I just argued, the media themselves serve as a conduit for rape culture is not a new idea: even as rape culture emerged as a powerful concept in second-wave feminism, its relationship to media culture was clear.[6] The very term "rape culture" was coined during that period, in the 1970s, and gained traction as feminist activists and thinkers started to recognize sexual violence as an outcome of patriarchal power, "a systemic problem that is institutionalized throughout the society."[7] This perspective radically revised traditional perceptions of instances of rape as isolated phenomena caused by deviant individuals enticed by blamable victims.

The reframing of rape as a systemic or structural problem was, even at the time, complicated by issues of race and class that were raised in the writings and speeches of women of color. The legal scholar Kimberlé Crenshaw crystallized these themes in a landmark essay, in which she pointed out that "the violence that many women experience is often shaped by other dimensions of their identities such as race and class;"[8] women of color experience sexual assault in ways that differ from how white women experience it. The neglect of racial and other factors, she argued, was another way of silencing survivors, as it "relegated the identity of women of color to a location that resists telling."[9] Thanks to these theorizations, the intersectionality of race, class, gender, and other identity markers is now an essential component of feminist approaches to rape culture, as well as to all aspects of culture and society.

The feminist scholar Ann Russo reminds us that race, class, sexual orientation, and other identity categories afford "differential access to a claim of innocence" in sexual assaults.[10] Her insight underscores how sexual assault survivors, unlike victims of other crimes, are automatically suspected of lying about their assaults. Skepticism about survivors' "innocence" also implies that they were somehow "guilty" or complicit in their own victimization. The idea that sexual violence survivors fabricate the stories of their assault is one among the many "rape myths" that form the building blocks of rape culture.

Feminist contemplation and theorization of sexual violence has identified a series of prevalent "rape myths," which are deeply embedded in many contemporary cultures and serve to undermine the credibility and capability of survivors.[11] As a consequence of these myths, rape is allowed to flourish as a social norm. A substantial body of feminist scholarship[12] has identified the following prevailing rape myths:

- Only "bad girls" get raped (which implies that survivors' behavior, clothing, sexual history, and attitude invite rape).
- Women enjoy rape (although this myth is largely gendered and not projected onto all survivors, it is nonetheless used in many contexts to rationalize rape).
- Survivors lie about being raped, especially if they have a grudge against the perpetrator.
- Survivors confuse "bad sex" with rape.

- If the survivor was drunk or used other judgment-impairing substances, the act was not rape.
- There is only one definition of rape: it is heterosexual, it involves penile–vaginal penetration, it is perpetrated by a male stranger on an unsuspecting woman, it involves the use of a weapon or considerable force, and it must be corroborated by evidence of resistance on the part of the female victim. This myth places responsibility for rape on the victim and eliminates the possibility of marital rape, rape by an acquaintance, same-sex rape, male rape, or rape of trans people; it also misses sexual violence that does not involve heterosexual intercourse. Although the US Department of Justice currently has a much more expansive and reasonable legal definition of rape,[13] this myth is still culturally prevalent in the United States and in many other societies.

Other rape myths refer specifically to racial and class stereotypes: "the placid Indian 'squaw' who readily gives her sexual favors, the passionate Black or mulatto woman who is always ready and sexually insatiable, the volatile Mexican woman who is fiery eyed and hot blooded, and the languid, opium-drowsed Asian woman whose only occupation is sex."[14] Racialized rape myths also specify what counts as a "credible" survivor and as a "credible" account of rape. In recent research, factors such as the race, class, gender, and sexual orientation of victims and perpetrators are found to play a significant role in the treatment of victims by the police, as well as in prosecutors' decisions as to whether to accept a case.[15] The ways in which race, class, sexual orientation, gender identity, and disability are used to discredit and trivialize sexual violence survivors leaves some of them with fewer legal protections than others and inhibits the reporting of sexual violence.

The silencing of sexual violence survivors as a result of the influence of rape myths is one of the most serious consequences of rape culture. Sexual assault survivors are reluctant to report for a range of reasons, many of which are related to fears created by rape myths. It is telling that such fears are reflected in studies across a wide range of countries and cultures, races and identities. Worldwide, a pitifully small percentage of sexual assaults are reported to the police or other authorities: the estimates of reported cases of sexual violence range from 5 to 25 percent of the number of actual cases.[16] Even for rich and famous white women in the global North, a culture of silence allowed multiple incidents of sexual assault, abuse, and harassment to continue unchecked for decades in some of the world's wealthiest corporations.

In the chapters that follow I will trace the specific strategies and structures of rape culture that harbored and hid sexual predation in the media industries, silencing the capacity of survivors to disclose their assaults. Delving into these processes requires a multifaceted analysis of the media environment: the workplace conditions that condone and conceal sexual violence, but also the mediated representations and images through which rape culture is circulated and interpreted and the ways in which the media—especially social media—have become a catalyst for silence breaking and for feminist activism against rape culture.

To think about media culture in this way frames it as a social apparatus in the sense defined by Michel Foucault: as an assemblage of interconnected images, discourses, laws, policies, philosophies, and other forms of social knowledge that operate strategically in the service of power.[17] Sexuality is, for Foucault, "a domain saturated with power,"[18] constructed through mechanisms such as religion, law, or the media, all of which claim to offer the "truth" about sex and thereby exert control over its meaning. The media are saturated with sex, as well as with sexual violence. In this book I explore how the media environment serves as a prime conduit for both silencing and silence breaking around rape culture.

Understanding the media environment involves paying close attention "to the production of culture, to the [media] texts themselves, and to their reception by the audience."[19] In conformity with this logic, the present book is divided into three chapters that address different facets of rape culture in the media, especially in terms of silencing and silence breaking. My starting point in chapter 1 is US media corporations, as these were the epicenter of the revelations that fueled the global spread of #MeToo and the current engagements with rape culture. Scrutinizing the media corporations in which rape culture ran rampant yet was deliberately hidden from view provides insight into the institutional framework of sexual predation at work. To say this is not to presume, blithely, that the way things happened at Fox News or in the Weinstein Company can be mapped directly onto a meatpacking plant in Iowa or a casino in Macao, even though those workplaces are just as likely to abet sexual violence. Plainly, that would be too easy a leap. But there is also evidence, given the rise of #MeToo/MeToo movements globally, that the sexual predation exposed in Hollywood and New York bridged systems and structures of workplaces in the United States and around the world. Sandra Pezqueda, a working-class Latina woman, observed in *TIME* magazine: "Someone who is in the limelight is able to speak out more easily than people who are poor. The reality of being a woman is the same—the difference is the risk each woman must take."[20] Those differential risks are, of course, significant; the life consequences—financial, familial, physical—are much greater and potentially more calamitous for poor women, women of color, lesbian women, transwomen.

This is even more alarming in light of the uptake of rape culture and endorsement of sexual violence, particularly against women, at the highest levels of political power, in parallel with the global rise of despotic populism.

The second chapter shifts the focus from organizational structures to media content, examining how rape culture has been systemically incorporated, resisted, and reinforced through representations, from pornography and sexual cybercrimes to news reporting. Some of these representations preceded and gave rise to the MeToo moment, some coincided with it and energized it, and some unfolded after #MeToo made its mark; some functioned to reassert silencing strategies, while some reinforced the structures that consolidate rape culture. My analyses center on forms of media that have had a global impact, from revenge porn to the work of the *Boston Globe*'s investigative "Spotlight" team.

The third chapter takes up the backlash against MeToo/#MeToo that has arisen after the hashtag went viral and runs from accusations of a "witch hunt" to intersectional critiques that challenge the movement's whiteness and its links to criminal justice systems that oppress marginalized and minoritized communities. These provocations and perceptions are important to the evolution and constant metamorphosis of MeToo and to the breaking of silences around rape culture.

The Brazilian educator and philosopher Paulo Freire writes of a "culture of silence" in situations of domination, where subordinate groups are rendered mute by those in power. Breaking this enforced and subjugating silence will, he believes, create the conditions for the oppressed to enter into dialogue with the oppressors, so that together they may create a vision for collective social change.[21]

#MeToo/MeToo called out the "culture of silence" that rape culture has imposed for centuries on sexual violence survivors. The silence has been broken. For all the ambivalences, tensions, and confrontations of the "MeToo moment," by breaking the silence, we are beginning to see our way toward transforming a rape culture.

Notes on Terminology

The MeToo/#MeToo movement's core concern is for survivors of sexual abuse, assault, and harassment, in the workplace as well as in other spaces and places. The term "survivor" has largely displaced "victim" in feminist writings on sexual assault; this is a consequence of the feminist conviction that those who experience sexual violence are never responsible for its occurrence. The sociologist Liz Kelly argued for the need to shift "the emphasis from viewing victims as passive victims of sexual violence to seeing them as active survivors."[22] While I concur completely with this view and support attributing to survivors of sexual abuse the overtones of courage, self-determination, and strength that attend the term "survivor," I find power in the term "victim" as well: the fact of victimization calls out the reality of a perpetrator, an assailant who deliberately sexually violated and harmed another being. "Survivor" seems to move past the harm done by the assault; "victim" re-centers it. In addition, not all people who are sexually attacked survive. In this book, while I use the term "survivor" most of the time, I use the word "victim" as well, not with a pejorative sense but to honor the fact that sexual violence causes harm and trauma. Sometimes I use "victim-survivor." This terminology speaks to my efforts to balance the recognition of survivors' spirit and strength with the real pain and injury of sexual violence, more clearly conveyed by "victim."

I have also grappled with how best to refer to the wide-ranging types of sexual violence that fall under the MeToo/#MeToo umbrella: catcalls and other forms of verbal harassment, unwanted touching, coercion, violent attacks, rape with objects, and the like. Legal definitions of "rape," "sexual abuse," "sexual battery," "sex offense," "harassment," and so on are specific and distinct, varying from state to state and from country to country and carrying with them particular penalties. As

I am not engaging in a formal legal analysis, the terms I use refer to commonly understood behaviors. One of the critiques of the #MeToo movement is its alleged lack of discernment about the differences between these behaviors, a critique that implies that some are less serious than others. The feminist journalist Jamie Utt calls this approach "perpetrator logic," as it discounts the survivor's experience of the impact of a sexual violation.[23] She rejects the notion of a continuum of sexual violence on a scale from negligible to serious and conceptualizes sexual violence instead as comprising "a matrix of intersecting behaviors" that can occur simultaneously and are all used to harm the victim. Similarly, Liz Kelly decades earlier pointed to "a basic common character" underpinning various forms of sexual violence.[24]

I am persuaded by their reasoning. Sexual violence doesn't usually happen in a clear-cut fashion, only one incident or form of sexual misconduct at a time, especially when the abuse is ongoing, as in a workplace or in a family setting. So, *pace* Utt, I use "sexual violence" as an umbrella term that encompasses abuse, assault, and harassment, occasionally substituting specific terms for a particular incident.

Following Kimberlé Crenshaw, I am committed "to the need to account for multiple grounds of identity when considering how the social world is constructed,"[25] especially with regard to sexual violence. Recognizing that racial classifications are constructed and often arbitrary, but nonetheless meaningful because of their history and cultural connotations, I use contemporary terms for racial categorizations: "African American" or "black," as the context requires; "white" for people of Caucasian descent; "Native American" or "Native" for indigenous peoples, specifying tribal membership whenever possible; particular Asian and South American national or subcultural classifications as appropriate.

As for gender, I similarly recognize the fluidity and constructedness of its categories. For brevity's sake, I use "woman" to designate any person who identifies as a woman, whether cis or trans or in any other way; and the same goes for "man." Following the terminology in the Human Rights Campaign report *A Time to Act*,[26] I use "trans" for anyone whose gender identity challenges traditional binary categories, including people who are nonbinary, gender fluid, genderqueer, gender diverse, or gender expansive.

Finally, my periodization of feminist thought and activism follows the "wave" model, in which the first wave corresponds to the period in the late nineteenth and early twentieth century most prominently defined by the women's suffrage movement in the United Kingdom and United States; the second wave spans the 1960s and 1970s, when feminism addressed a range of social and sexual rights; and the third wave begins in the 1990s, being marked by a focus on greater inclusivity, and also by the reclamation of "girl culture." The second wave marked the emergence of global feminisms as well: the first World Conference on Women was held in Mexico City in 1975. It is clear that the waves were not distinct; they overlapped in many respects. It is also true that this model discounts the activism of women of color that predated the suffrage movement. It might elide the diversity of subsequent feminist activism, too. With rueful acknowledgment of its inadequacy, I rely on the wave metaphor as a good shorthand for the timeframe and general theme of feminist activism.

1
Rapacity

Monsters, Inc.

The real and radicalizing fury at the heart of the #MeToo movement was inflamed, in part, by the fact that we knew and admired—even loved—the men who betrayed us so: the genial and jocular Bill Cosby, whose portrayal of Heathcliff Huxtable defined devoted fatherhood; the charming, dimpled Matt Lauer, whose celebrity interviews were as invigorating a start to the day as a strong cup of coffee; the Grammy Award-winning hip-hop artist R. Kelly, whose songs enlivened weddings and parties; the brooding genius Harvey Weinstein, who entranced us with cinematic gems such as Shakespeare in Love and Good Will Hunting. The list goes on, of course, in what Carina Chocano has described as "a carnival of exposure" where "we've watched the stones overturned to reveal more and more supposedly great men as criminals, perverts or frauds."[1]

It's worth noting that almost all of these "great men" worked in the US media industries, either on- or off-screen. While women of color were aware that Tarana Burke had mobilized grassroots activism around the issues of sexual abuse and harassment at least a decade earlier, the rallying cry of MeToo exploded into a powerful global social movement only after these American male media figures were publicly identified as sexual predators.

A key factor in the phenomenon was the shock generated by the revelations of our media heroes' metamorphosis from good guys into ghouls. These men had risen to the top of their professions and were acclaimed as role models and superstars. But their charismatic public façades concealed hearts of darkness, secret lives of depravity and deceit. Their reported transgressions evoke ancient tales of shape-shifters and werewolves—seemingly respectable humans who transform at will into craven beasts capable of brutal savagery.

In fact the metaphor of the monster has come up frequently in the narratives of women who were attacked by these men. In her autobiography, the actor Rose McGowan referred to Harvey Weinstein only as "the Monster;"[2] the actor Salma Hayek declared: "Harvey Weinstein is my monster, too;"[3] the artist and model Barbara Bowman said of Bill Cosby: "He is a monster. He came at me like a monster."[4] The anthropologist David Gilmore observes that monsters represent "human qualities that have to be repudiated, externalized and defeated, the most important of which are aggression and sexual sadism, that is, id forces."[5]

On his account, monsters "live in borderline places … parallel to and intersecting the human community."[6] They erupt into human lives out of nowhere, wreaking destruction and causing mayhem. Most frighteningly, they walk among us undetected, waiting for the opportunity to ambush an unsuspecting victim.

We are chillingly aware now that sexual predators hide in plain sight in our workplaces, our schools, our hospitals, our churches, our neighborhoods, and our homes; they are our colleagues, supervisors, mentors, teachers, priests, doctors, relatives, and friends. Their presence and their predations are not new: women, children, trans and nonbinary people, and even some men have been molested and harassed by clandestine sex criminals for years, even for centuries. But our public recognition of these offenses and our public confrontations of them and challenges to them are relatively recent, having been galvanized by the media men whose iniquities set off the social media storms that grew into an anti-rape revolution.

#MeToo was prompted by the burgeoning revelations of serial sexual assault by Hollywood movie mogul Harvey Weinstein. At the same time, Pulitzer Prize-winning reporting carried out by the *New York Times* and the *New Yorker* magazine documented Weinstein's long history of sexual predation, and that story was bookended by mediated callouts of other media celebrities—Cosby, Lauer, Ailes, Kelly, and many others. These men were all based in the United States, but because of the global interconnections of the contemporary media environment they were well known in many other countries, and exposés of them as sexual offenders hit the headlines the world over. Even as these revelations were unfurling, media men in various nations and regions were also being identified as sexual predators: the BBC's Jimmy Savile, Canadian radio host Jian Ghomeshi, Indian Bollywood star Nana Patekar, Japanese television reporter Noriyuki Yamaguchi, and Mexican television director Gustavo Loza, to name just a few. The ferment in the media industries was the epicenter of the ensuing spillover of reports of sexual assault, abuse, and harassment in practically every industry and every aspect of contemporary life.

It is indisputable that sexual assaults and harassment occur in virtually every profession, because gendered and sexual power dynamics characterize every workplace; it is also true that many powerful institutions, including prestigious universities and the Catholic Church, have deliberately moved to cover up decades of atrocious sex crimes. But in media organizations the structures of gender, sex, and power that enable these situations tend to be very close to the surface, particularly in areas such as television and film. In these industries, not only is patriarchal power firmly entrenched, but the beauty myth—as Naomi Wolf dubbed it[7]—determines careers, especially for women. The fact that the initial wave of #MeToo outcries was entirely from women who named male perpetrators signals a need to rigorously examine the specific structures, processes, and practices that create contexts in which men can enact gender violence with apparent impunity.

This is not to say, of course, that all men are sexual predators, or that all men who work in the media industries espouse predation. On the contrary, many media men have worked actively to uncover and address these crimes, for example the journalist Ronan Farrow, whose reporting of the Weinstein allegations won a Pulitzer Prize for public service. Men, and people of all genders, are allies in the battle against sexual violence. And, of course, not all sexual assault survivors or victims are women. With this caveat, it is still important to acknowledge that the dynamics of gender and sexuality in media (especially television and film) industries are archetypal in terms of emphasized heterosexuality and retrograde gender roles, and in this respect these industries provide a strong analytical site in which it is possible to examine the power systems that give rise to sexual harassment, assault, and abuse at work in other contexts. This is borne out by the fact that a much higher percentage of women experience sexual harassment and assault in the media industries than in any other white-collar profession.[8]

I will begin here with some key questions that have driven public discourse on the sexual misconduct of men at the top of media professions. First, why did these men repeatedly engage in sexual aggressions against the women in their workplaces? And, second, how did organizational systems and structures enable this sexual misconduct to recur, without acknowledgment or redress, over the span of years, even decades?

It would be easy to dismiss these sexual assaults as individual aberrations, isolated acts to be chalked up to personality problems. Yet the frequency and scope of such behaviors call for a different level of analysis. The very similarity of pattern across the assaults reported via #MeToo speaks to the existence of a systemic framework that gave rise to, and sustained, these crimes. The findings can give us insights into the wide range of work environments in which such violations occur. This is not to claim that all workplaces and cultural contexts are the same, but to point out that identifying the organizational elements that tacitly condone sexual violence at work offers us a way to see past individual instances into the broader mobilizing structures.

Feminist scholarship on rape and sexual assault recognizes that so-called sex crimes are not simply about sex: they are driven and defined by a complex intersection of sex, violence, power, culture, and politics. Not all rapes are committed by men, but both contemporary data and the historical evidence show clearly that, overall, most perpetrators are male, while most victims and survivors are female. One of the earliest studies of rape in society noted that rape is largely "a male prerogative … man's basic weapon of force against woman, the principal agent of his will and her fear."[9] Men are not hard-wired to rape: rather, rape and other forms of sexual and gender-based violence are outcomes of patriarchal power systems. The legal scholar Catharine MacKinnon defines rape as a crime of gender inequality rooted in power hierarchies that typically lead to the domination of women by men.[10] A 2006 United Nations report noted that all forms of violence against women, including sexual violence, result from unequal power relations between men and women and are a "key means through which male control over women's agency and sexuality is maintained."[11] Societies with high rates of sexual violence against women are "characterized by male dominance, gender-role rigidity and glorification of warfare."[12] And in most societies "men continue to grow up with, and are socialized into, a deeply misogynistic, male-dominated culture, where violence against women—from the subtle to the homicidal—is disturbingly common. It's *normal.*"[13]

Sexual dominance is a manifestation of power. It is important to emphasize, again, that not all men are rapists, nor are all rapists men: there is no causal relationship between sex or gender and sexual violence. Rather, sexual violence is one outcome of a gendered hierarchy that sets up patriarchal power and defines it by the criterion of violence.

The high-profile media men identified by the MeToo movement as serial rapists held tremendous institutional, social, and economic power, even "godlike standing."[14] The creative industries, of which film and television are an important sector, are marked by unequal distributions of power whereby a small number of people hold an inordinate amount of power and men rank high, occupying most of the executive and decision-making positions. One analysis of news companies that covers 59 nations and 522 organizations found that men hold 75 percent of the top executive and board positions.[15] The annual Celluloid Ceiling report, which tracks women's employment in film and television, found that women comprise "only 20% of all directors, writers, producers, editors, and cinematographers working on the 250 top-grossing films" worldwide, and only 1 percent of all films employ more than 10 women in these roles.[16] "If you look at the *Hollywood Reporter* most powerful women's list, every one of those women still reports to a man," noted that magazine's former editor Janice Min.[17]

The prominence and dominance of men at high levels of the media industries has serious implications for sexual misconduct. This is largely due to the fact that institutional and structural power operate along gendered lines, enabling sexual predators—typically male—to dominate and abuse women without repercussions. Of course, the gender roles are occasionally reversed—women may harass or sexually assault men, or men may sexually harass other men—but these scenarios are far less common than male-on-female attacks. While "all adult women are culturally identified as potential targets of sexual harassment," the few men who report experiencing it tend not to conform to stereotypical masculine performance or are disempowered because they are young or low-ranking.[18] Again, power differentials coupled with gender hierarchies are the main catalytic factors in sexual harassment and assault in the workplace.

*

Men in powerful positions have long used social status both as license to commit acts of sexual violence against women and as protection from penalties. The historical phrase droit du seigneur ('the nobleman's right') or *ius primae noctis* ('the right of the first night') designates a presumptive right of highborn men to be granted sexual access to women of lower social status on their wedding night. The historian Laura Betzig writes: "'Noble' men in most 'civilized' societies have had exclusive sexual access to more than one woman in their own households; and they have had privileged sexual access to women in other men's households."[19] Although there has been some debate about the reality of the droit du seigneur, many scholars confirm its de facto existence, in some form, in many cultures and regions. Whatever its origins, "the seignorial right of prelibation is simply an abuse of force and good pleasure."[20]

The workplace hierarchy parallels a manorial or seigneurial system in that it grants high-ranking men tremendous power and privilege over other employees. This organizational structure is especially obvious in the film and television industries, which were the site of the first #MeToo revelations. Like the medieval seigneurs, the high-status male predators in these industries understood their power to be not only economic and legal but also sexual. This form of entitlement—sexual entitlement—provides insight into why Harvey Weinstein, Bill Cosby, and other men who had attained star status in the media industries routinely subjected female colleagues to sexual assault and harassment.

Psychological entitlement is "a relatively stable belief that one should receive desirable treatment with little consideration of deservingness"[21] and be "treated as special or unique in social settings."[22] The business ethicist Valerie Rosenblatt notes that socially dominant people in organizations often feel "that they are more entitled to the use of power at the expense of others to get ahead and maintain their dominant positions."[23] A growing body of scholarship on workplace psychopathy indicates that entitlement, taken in this sense, is characteristic of psychopathic personalities in senior management of organizations; the research also indicates that in the upper ranks of corporations the base rate of psychopathy may be three times as high as in the general population.[24] Interestingly, some of the characteristics of psychopathic personalities, such as self-confidence and interpersonal dominance, are perceived to be traits of effective leadership and facilitate workplace success. However, "such individuals are often destructive leaders in the long term."[25]

As psychopathy comprises a cluster of personality traits, it is important to note that not all high-ranking men displaying such characteristics engage in aggressive or assaultive behavior. On the other hand, those who do are likely to have high levels of entitlement, especially with regard to masculinity and sex roles. Prosecuting attorney Joan Illuzzi-Orbon summed up this sense of sexual entitlement by describing Harvey Weinstein's belief that women "want to be in this universe [and] the universe is run by me and they don't get to complain when they're stepped on or demoralized or raped and abused."[26]

In general, men with more traditional views of masculinity, where manhood is defined in terms of strength, status, confidence, and aggression, are more likely to exhibit hostility to women, rape-supportive attitudes, and sexually coercive or violent behavior.[27] These traditionally masculine traits are also connected with feelings of both masculine entitlement and sexual entitlement. Masculine entitlement refers to the belief that men "are superior by social definition" and therefore can expect to get "whatever one wants";[28] that men's needs take precedence over women's;[29] and that women are responsible for gratifying these needs. Sexual entitlement goes one step further along the view that men "have strong sexual needs that must be satisfied ... that men, in general, are entitled to act out their impulses."[30] Numerous studies link sexual entitlement to rape.[31] The sociologist Michael Kimmel points out that "though both men and women feel entitled to [sexual] pleasure ... men still believe that that entitlement also covers acting on it—even when the woman doesn't want to."[32] Given that entitlement is a marker of high-status men in work environments, it is evident that men in such positions see sexual access to women as a given, a job perk, and their workplaces tacitly but actively support such attitudes.

In her groundbreaking work, the feminist legal scholar Catharine MacKinnon argues that men's material power shapes their attitudes to the issue of sexual access to women in the workplace. She writes: "Economic power is to sexual harassment as physical power is to rape."[33] The prominent US media men accused of sexual misconduct had egregious levels of economic power: not only did they earn astronomical salaries, but they generated huge revenues for the companies that employed them. Matt Lauer, according to *Esquire*, was "a marquee draw that earned the [NBC] network hundreds of millions per year."[34] Harvey Weinstein's annual salary was upward of $2.5 million, with additional benefits such as $500,000 a year for private air travel, and under his leadership the Weinstein Company grossed as much as $500 million a year at the box office.[35] Bill O'Reilly of Fox News earned a salary of $20 million a year, was "the top-rated host in cable news," and had "made Fox News a ratings powerhouse."[36] Les Moonves, the CEO of CBS, was "one of the most powerful media executives in America" and "earned nearly seventy million dollars," which made him "one of the highest paid corporate executives in the world."[37] Their earning power marked them as invaluable to the operations of their companies.

This framework of gender, power, and entitlement in organizations indicates the likelihood that these men felt they had a right of sexual access to the women in their workplaces. This preposterous (but theoretically tenable) belief may have been exacerbated by yet another aspect of the sexual dynamics at work: the requirements for many women to be sexualized in the performance of their jobs. At Fox News, for example, women were pressured to wear heavy "beauty pageant" makeup, short skirts, high heels, and body-hugging clothing.[38] CEO Roger Ailes was known to have an "obsession" with women's legs, arranging studio sets so that a "leg cam" blatantly focused on female news anchors' legs.[39] *TIME* magazine reported that Ailes "hand-picked blonde skinny women for on-camera shows ... and demanded their desks be see-through so that the audience could see their legs."[40]

Male Fox News employees, of course, endured no such constraints on their dress or working conditions. The strictures were imposed on women by Ailes and other high-ranking men, who later cost 21st Century Fox over $80 million in landmark sexual harassment settlements brought by numerous women. The media industries also sexualize actors and models, whose jobs frequently require the projection of conventional modes of representing female sexuality. "Because I was a woman," writes the actor Rose McGowan, "I was considered to be an owned object. I was sold for the pleasure of the public. Deeply programmed men (and women) made money selling my breasts, my skin, my hair, my emotions, my health, my being ... 'Cause you know, if strange men masturbate to your movies, you must be of some value. Sounds like a sex worker, right?"[41]

As a consequence, when McGowan consulted a criminal attorney about her assault by Weinstein, she was told that she would have no credibility because she had acted in a sex scene.[42] The journalist Lizzie Feidelson reflects that "sex scenes are ripe ... for deliberate abuses of power,"[43] most of which target women. After filing a police complaint about Weinstein, the lingerie model and actor Ambra Battilana Gutierrez was publicly smeared in the media for that work, with invented claims that she was a prostitute.[44] Lingerie ads tend to be read as supporting traditional sexual dynamics in which women are sexually objectified, because "one of the key functions of lingerie is the impact it has on men."[45] In reality, it takes two people to engage in a heterosexual sex scene, and one of them is male; male models also bare their bodies to make a living in advertising. But men are not shamed or discredited for such work, while women's engagement in these activities is interpreted as a sign of their sexual turpitude and exploited to diminish their standing and credibility.

This is not to suggest that women's dress or behavior in any way invites or justifies sexual attacks; nor is it to blame these women for the abuse to which they were subjected. Rather it is to point out that a gendered double standard existed in these media workplaces that positioned women's sexuality differently from men's. Female sexuality was objectified, used to create a gendered role that disempowered women. The double standard clearly conveyed that men had more power and freedom in these workplaces than women and that, to use John Berger's famous phrase, "men act and women appear."[46] Per MacKinnon's analysis, women "are required to market sexual attractiveness to men, who tend to hold the economic power and position to enforce their predilections."[47] She continues: "The point is that it is the very qualities which men find sexually attractive in the women they harass that are the real qualifications for the jobs for which they hire them."[48] In fact, one Fox News employee reported of Roger Ailes that, "if he was thinking of hiring a woman, he'd ask himself if he would fuck her, and if he would, then he'd hire her to be on-camera."[49] For women in the media (and other) industries, there are great economic benefits to enacting stereotypical sexiness and serious economic risks to abandoning it, but at the same time this performance is seized on by predatory men as an ostensible entitlement to sex.

Even within work environments where sexualization was a condition of employment for women but not for men, women viewed their work relationships with high-ranking men as purely professional. Recognizing this, the men took advantage of women's expectations of mentorship or career advice to exploit and pervert ostensibly professional interactions. For example, many of the women who survived Bill Cosby's rapes say he assaulted them after auditions or photo shoots or dinner invitations they thought were career-related. The actor Heidi Thomas recounts: "I had the understanding I was going to be receiving private acting coaching from him. This was the opportunity of a lifetime. A driver would pick me up, my agent was paying for it. That made it all very, very professional." But instead, when Thomas arrived at his home, Cosby drugged and raped her.[50] An intern at Epic Records reported that the label's star hip-hop artist R. Kelly treated her "as his personal sex object."[51] Laurie Luhn, a Fox employee who aspired to work in political communication, was sexually assaulted, first at a job interview and then repeatedly for decades after she was hired by Roger Ailes.[52]

These predatory men were opportunists, and their media workplaces obligingly handed them opportunities to prey on unsuspecting and disempowered women. Their predations were sometimes even rewarded: at CBS, for example, "men accused of sexual harassment were promoted, even as the company paid settlements to women with complaints."[53]

The hypersexual gender roles and power structures of the television and film industries provide a crystal-clear view into how organizations serve as hosts for predators, just as certain organisms harbor and cultivate parasites. This is tantamount to a rape culture. The consolidation of male power and privilege that supported cultures of sexual entitlement at Fox News, NBC, CBS, and Miramax is germane to what we'll find in any industry or workplace with a similar history and gender hierarchy—and most contemporary organizations tend to fall into this category. Indeed, #MeToo precipitated revelations of sexual assault, abuse, and harassment in a range of workplaces, in the United States and elsewhere: women are speaking now about sexual violence in fields such as agricultural labor, medicine, food services, engineering, politics, the hospitality industries, and in myriad other occupations. Organizational rape culture rests on gender power structures that enable sexual entitlement, usually male sexual entitlement, and normalize it. In addition, workplaces enable powerful and entitled men to hire women they find desirable, and then to act on that perception.

So, when the actor Alyssa Milano tweeted, in 2017, "[i]f all women who have been sexually harassed or assaulted wrote 'Me too' as a status, we might give people a sense of the magnitude of the problem," it struck a deep chord with women in a multitude of other professions and places who had until then been silenced.

The MeToo movement has broken centuries of silence around the issues of sexual assault and harassment. But this silence was far from volitional. As a routine practice, organizations not only condoned sexual predation but actively *silenced* survivors of sexual harassment and abuse in the workplace. In the next section I will address the way mechanisms of silencing in media industries served to protect male sexual entitlement, cultivate rape culture, and effectively subvert the possibility of solidarity among survivors.

Danger Zones

As revelations of gender violence and sexual misconduct by media men continue to unfurl, it is becoming increasingly clear that many people were already acutely aware of the predators who lurked in their workplaces, often wielding considerable power and prestige. When women were attacked—in offices and hotel rooms, in hallways and studios—agents and staff people urged them to remain silent; corporate lawyers arranged for "hush money" settlements; secretaries and personal assistants continued to facilitate dangerous liaisons with the same men. When attempts were made to report these behaviors, swift steps were taken to quell or discount the female accusers. At a deeper level, it became clear that the "secrets" of sexual abuse had long been guarded by a webwork of strategic mechanisms braced by gendered power differentials.

Among the women who worked with them, these male predators were known as danger zones. "Everybody knew that Matt Lauer was having inappropriate relationships with women," said a *Today* show producer quoted on the entertainment blog *The Wrap*.[54] According to the *New York Times*, "[d]ozens of Mr. Weinstein's former and current employees, from assistants to top executives, said they knew of inappropriate conduct while they worked for him. Only a handful said they ever confronted him."[55] Barbara Bowman, who was repeatedly raped by Bill Cosby, lamented: "The women victimized by Bill Cosby have been talking about his crimes for more than a decade."[56] In fact, when the comedian Hannibal Buress publicly condemned Bill

Cosby as a rapist, he exhorted audiences to google "Bill Cosby rape" to confirm how widely known his assaults were. An external review of the NPR newsroom where Senior VP Michael Oreskes harassed women noted the existence of a "whisper network" among the female news staff regarding his untoward behaviors.[57] The sexual misdeeds of the PBS and CBS host Charlie Rose were also common knowledge.[58] But such behaviors went unchecked and unreported for the most part; they were implicitly condoned and collusively ignored by organizations and authorities, and this gave men tacit license to continue to accost women.

Dozens of women who never reported their assaults have now broken the silence, to recount the feelings of intimidation, fear, and guilt that prevented them from disclosing those incidents. The actor Salma Hayek detailed both Harvey Weinstein's harassment and her silence, which stemmed from the notion that she was a "nobody" along with her desperate ambition to finish directing and starring in the feminist movie *Frida*.[59] The actor Lupita Nyong'o said she blamed herself for Weinstein's behavior and was silent for fear of "not being believed and instead being ridiculed."[60] The actor Asia Argento, who was assaulted by Weinstein, said she did not speak out for fear that he would "crush" her and destroy her career.[61] A former NBC producer explained that Matt Lauer attacked women in his workplace "within his stable, where he exerted power, and he knew people wouldn't ever complain."[62] A *60 Minutes* reporter, Habiba Nosheen, was threatened by CBS that she would not work in television again unless she withdrew a federal sexual harassment complaint and signed a corporate nondisclosure agreement.[63]

Women's silence resulted from "the fear of retaliation, of being blackballed, of being fired from a job they can't afford to lose."[64] The men in question used the professional context, as well as their power within media industries, to exploit women's career ambitions and to use them in enforcing the silence of the survivors. Time and again, women were discredited as liars and vamps. Disclosing dark secrets carried such serious risks and potential penalties that silence seemed to be the only option, even as the patriarchal corporate apparatus was fully cognizant of these so-called secrets and operated to enforce their concealment.

The phrase "open secret" is an oxymoron, and hence a paradox, precisely because the secret is not really a secret; the terms of its nondisclosure are predicated on a delicate balance of power. In the case of workplace sexual assault, this power balance is usually gendered. For women, the risks of disclosure pertain to employment and career trajectories—but the risks of nondisclosure are also great, in that more women will be physically endangered as a result.

The risks of disclosure are similarly serious for corporations, so much so that settlements and legal actions that protect male predators are deemed to be worth making in order to ensure the continued success of the enterprise. For survivors of sexual assault, nondisclosure agreements are a deal with the devil. For all those who collude in preserving the open secret, the balance of acknowledged disclosure and legal nondisclosure normalizes sexual misconduct and sustains a profitable organizational culture.

"Secrecy and risk are closely connected," notes the anthropologist Graham M. Jones. "Secrecy engenders risk insofar as concealment entails the possibility of unwelcome revelation; noncirculation also creates risks of its own, such as the breakdown of social relations or cultural reproduction."[65] Certainly a workplace culture is created when sexual assault becomes an open secret that is preserved through complexly interrelated mechanisms, which range from individual fear to executive-level decisions and legal actions. In such a culture, violence against women functions to destabilize women's work environment, reasserting the precariousness of women's labor by rendering female bodies vulnerable to attack and leaving them without any means of recourse. In a sense, such violence is the ultimate "feminization" of labor; as Donna Haraway has written, "[t]o be feminized means to be made extremely vulnerable; able to be disassembled, reassembled, exploited … leading an existence that always borders on the obscene, out of place, and reducible to sex."[66]

The secrets of sexual predation sometimes travel among women through "whisper networks," but the subterranean routes of these networks sustain the erasure of reality. The dark sexual secrets of workplace gender violence are borne by individual women who experience them physically and emotionally, and yet the violence percolates throughout the organization and ultimately into society, preserving the gender order. In addition, not everyone is privy to the network: women of color, women in the lower ranks of the organization, trans or nonbinary people may not have access to the whispers. Thus the open secret of workplace sexual assault is exposed as a mechanism for social control.

Rape culture is generally understood to be constituted through public discourses, media representations, legal frameworks, societal norms and mores, and gender ideologies.[67] But silence, too, is a defining characteristic of rape culture.

Most sexual assaults are not reported, for a range of reasons that include survivors' feelings of shame or self-blame, fear of social stigmatization and retaliation, concerns about credibility and consequent redress, and a lack of reporting mechanisms or options. "Victims of sexual assault are already subjected to a state of intimidation and violence and have felt a loss of control caused by the assault," explains the feminist legal scholar Gabrielle Lucero. "On top of those effects, victims must also face rape culture that normalizes sexual assault and blames victims for their own assault. … Sexual assault leaves victims in fear, and rape culture further perpetuates those fears and prevents them from reporting their assault."[68]

Sexual assault survivors are thus discouraged from reporting their experiences through an acute sense of the risks, repercussions, and recalcitrance they are likely to encounter, even if such consequences are not overtly articulated. Social mores and institutional intransigence create a climate in which reporting sexual assault is at best discounted and at worst punitive for the survivor, whom it retraumatizes. This socially sanctioned silencing is at once caused by and contributory to rape culture.

Within media organizations where sexual harassment

and assault occurred unchecked over long periods of time, survivors' silence was tacitly imposed for the same reasons as in broader society. But it is crucial to recognize that, even beyond the tendency of survivors themselves to remain silent, silencing was a finely calibrated method built into the official operations of media enterprises. In these circumstances, the acts of keeping the silence within these organizational systems were strategic acts: they were contrived through practice and policy and were essential to the conduct of business as usual, which included routine sexual harassment.

Such an organizational culture is one medium that breeds rape culture.

I describe the silence imposed by organizations on women survivors as "strategic" because it was constructed by design, to protect not only the organizations but their predatory employees and entrenched cultures of toxic misogyny. "Silence is strategic," writes the rhetorician Barry Brummett, "when someone has pressing reason to speak but does not."[69] As a system, the organizations had pressing reason to speak on behalf of their female employees so as to create a safe and productive work environment, but they engineered strategies for not doing so. As victims of sexual abusers in the workplace, the women had pressing reason to speak in order to stop the abuses and improve their work situations, but they did not, because the organizational systems in place specifically prevented them from publicly revealing the misconduct. "Allowing victims to speak out is a necessary form of prevention," notes the lawyer Vasundhara Prasad, "because it exposes patterns of abuse, warns those who might become victims, and encourages others similarly situated to come forward with their own claims."[70]

Yet when women in media organizations tried to report sexual assaults and other malfeasance, they were thwarted by various means, which ranged from tactics designed to deter or discredit survivors to legal actions that muzzled formal charges.

Often the first impediment to disclosure was the absence of a clear avenue for reporting incidents confidentially. Thus the actor Eliza Dushku, who received a $9.5 million settlement from CBS after being sexually harassed on the set of a TV show, said she knew of no "safe person you could go to" with her complaints; she also expressed anxiety about losing her job if she reported the harassment—and she was in fact fired after she approached her harasser to express her concerns.[71] Similarly, despite repeated allegations that the R&B artist R. Kelly had had sexual relationships with underage girls, his record label denied any responsibility. The former CEO of Jive Records, Barry Weiss, said that the musician's criminal behavior "was none of his business,"[72] and the label's attorneys argued that Kelly's "alleged tortious conduct" had "nothing to do" with the record company.[73] Thus, while acknowledging Kelly's behavior, the record label provided no corporate reporting mechanism for his victims. Employees of the Weinstein Company described the human resources office as "a sham, a place where complaints went to die."[74] Reports made there were not confidential: Weinstein was informed about them. In addition, in many media workplaces, women were blamed for the abuses they experienced and were offered no recourse. A woman who complained about an assault by the Canadian Broadcasting Company radio host Jian Ghomeshi was advised to "make this a less toxic workplace" for herself; another was told to "work around it."[75] The deliberate obfuscation and sabotage of employees' reporting channels and the abandonment of institutional accountability for the actions of predatory male employees were the first steps taken to silence injured women.

Smear campaigns that undermined women's credibility were a second potent silencing mechanism. After the actor and model Ambra Gutierrez filed a police report against Harvey Weinstein for sexually molesting her, tabloid newspapers began publishing lurid accounts of her having worked as a prostitute in Italy. The stories, which Gutierrez maintains are false, appear to have been sourced by an intelligence firm hired by Weinstein. The tabloids also published photographs of Gutierrez modeling lingerie. "[J]ust because I was a lingerie model or whatever, I had to be in the wrong," Gutierrez said. "I had people telling me, 'Maybe it was how you dressed'"[76]—a classic case of victim blaming. She believes her career was ruined by this negative publicity. Women who complained of sexual harassment at Fox News were smeared by the organization's public relations staff, who falsely claimed "that their ratings were low, that they weren't hacking it, they were lazy, they were alcoholics, they were drug addicts."[77] Many of these women could not find employment in the television industry after filing harassment claims. Threats of personal defamation and professional retaliation deterred many women from speaking out, especially when they saw the real consequences that this had on their colleagues who did.

These tactics were covert and unofficial moves made by organizations—but most of these media corporations also silenced women overtly and legally, by dint of contractual processes, forced arbitration clauses, and formal out-of-court settlements guarded by draconian nondisclosure agreements (NDAs).

One little-known silencing mechanism was the use of the "catch and kill" strategy. The "kill fee" has long been a standard clause in journalistic contracts, especially in freelance work. A kill fee is a payment given to a journalist as compensation for a story that a media outlet decides not to publish. Normally, if a story is contracted and then "killed" by a publication, the rights revert to the author, who can then try to sell it elsewhere. But the media juggernaut American Media Inc.—owner of the *National Enquirer*, of *OK!*, and of other tabloid outlets—engaged in paying sources, including survivors, for their stories about celebrity men's sexual misconduct and subsequently killing these stories in order to quell the report and protect the men.[78] What is more, David Pecker, the CEO of AMI, told Donald Trump's attorney that "he could buy the rights to problematic stories and prevent them from being published."[79]

In the spirit of sharing open secrets and alerting women to predatory men, in 2017 the journalist Moira Donegan compiled the "Shitty Media Men" spreadsheet, listing the names of men who worked in the media industries and had been identified by women as sexual predators. Donegan had intended "Shitty

Media Men" to be shared only among friends, but it quickly leaked and went viral, gaining entries from a spiraling list of anonymous users. The list had the caveat that it was based on rumors and hearsay, but it led to defamation lawsuits filed against Donegan that have yet to be adjudicated. Defamation suits can have a chilling effect on disclosures of sexual assault or harassment and are often filed with the explicit goal of silencing survivors or intimidating them into dropping their claims. Such suits employ tactics known in legal circles as DARVO: deny, attack, and reverse victim and offender. Some of these suits are, of course, legitimate responses to false allegations, but research indicates that false reporting is quite rare.[80] Because claims must be handled at an individual rather than a societal or cultural level, they raise the historically problematic issues of assessing the survivors' credibility, questioning their consent, and endlessly replaying the sexual assault scenarios in ways that can be retraumatizing. The "he said, she said" standoffs are about vilification—usually of the survivor—rather than about virtue.

Even more effective official strategies are nondisclosure agreements (NDAs) and mandatory arbitration clauses. These policies not only derail criminal trials but prevent women from speaking about their abuse at any point, even to therapists or family members. In fact all the Weinstein Company's contracts contained nondisparagement clauses that expressly forbade employees from making *any* criticism of the company or its executives if that could harm its "business reputation" or "any employee's personal reputation."[81] But, beyond this blanket ban, specific complaints of sexual harassment were handled with swift cash settlements and NDAs, with no penalty to Weinstein. The same holds for Fox News, NBC, and CBS and for the entertainers R. Kelly and Bill Cosby. In many cases, the out-of-court settlements added up to tens of millions of dollars over long periods of time. For example, at Fox News $45 million was paid over decades to Roger Ailes's many sexual harassment victims,[82] while $32 million was paid out for Bill O'Reilly's misconduct.[83] Bill Cosby paid former Temple University staffer Andrea Constand $3.38 million in a secret settlement when she brought a 2006 civil case against him for sexual assault;[84] other women witnesses could not testify and were required to remain anonymous, identified only as "Jane Does."[85] R. Kelly paid hundreds of thousands of dollars to teenage girls to settle lawsuits that claimed inappropriate sexual contact with them.[86]

In most cases, the accused men retained their highly paid positions for years—and, even when they were let go, their severance packages often exceeded the amounts of the settlements. The women were bound to silence, which had long-term effects on their well-being. Rowena Chiu, a former Weinstein assistant, described signing a 30-page settlement agreement under conditions of extreme duress, after she and her colleague Zelda Perkins brought suit against Harvey Weinstein. The NDA prevented them from speaking to anyone, even to each other, about the rape Chiu had experienced. "I suffered," she wrote, "completely isolated from those who could have provided the support I needed: a loved one, a trusted pastor, a respected therapist—even the man I would marry."[87] She described suicide attempts and depression, characteristics of post-rape trauma. Other women report similar effects. Ambra Gutierrez, also forced to sign an NDA after she was molested by Weinstein, similarly experienced severe depression and felt mentally and physically "destroyed" by the assault and her enforced silence about it.[88]

NDAs are about secrecy, but they also point to the notion of an "open secret," as their purpose is to prevent the disclosure of an *acknowledged* incident of misconduct. The crafting of an NDA involves legal counsel, human resources personnel, top executives, and the parties involved in the incident, so the "secret" is a credited fact that has been affirmed and is deliberately being expunged from the record by the organization. NDAs legalize and formalize the knowledge of what must remain forever publicly unknown, even if the object of the NDA is, informally, an "open" secret. These agreements thus constitute a pivot point of simultaneous disclosure and nondisclosure, transparency and secrecy. The contradictions and illogic inherent in this kind of construct capture the organizational culture in which NDAs and open secrets are prevalent, especially with regard to workplace sexual misconduct.

The phrase "toxic misogyny" has been used to describe the work environments at Fox News and at CBS under CEO Les Moonves. These workplaces were danger zones, where women were ambushed, assaulted, and professionally undermined by men who flourished despite—or even because of—their malfeasance. "Elements of sexual character are embedded in the distinctive sets of practices sometimes called 'occupational cultures,'" notes the sociologist R. W.

Connell.[89] The deliberate and systemic silencing of women's experiences of sexual abuse and harassment clearly indicate that these offenses were deeply imbricated into the cultures of the media organizations in which they occurred.

Recognizing the harms associated with silencing reports of workplace wrongdoing, some US states are considering bills to ban NDAs. The logic behind the proposed legislation acknowledges "that the bargaining imbalance between the employer and the employee gives too much power to an employer who can turn a blind eye toward abuses in the workplace, leaving the employee with no way of seeking justice."[90] Legal scholars, too, are critiquing the ethics and enforceability of NDAs, recognizing that sexual assault survivors did not commit any wrongdoing and so are unfairly penalized if they speak out after signing an NDA; in addition, NDAs impede the social benefits that could accrue from survivors' testimony. While at times NDAs are voluntarily entered into by all parties and can protect survivors from unwanted publicity and stigma, it is also clear "that these agreements can be weaponized to keep abusers hidden from public scrutiny."[91] These secret settlements, which were once viewed as the only way to deal with the competing interests of sexual assault survivors and corporations, are only now beginning to be recognized as "a societal toxin or contagion—the kind of threat about which others should be warned."[92]

The repeated, often decades-long trail of male sexual misconduct that was deliberately silenced by media organizations is also a reminder that gender regimes within a workplace depend on and reinforce specific sex–power roles. For the sexual harassment of women to endure as an unspoken workplace norm, a gender hierarchy that privileges and protects dominant masculinity has to be built into the organizational culture. This is accomplished through the maintenance of everyday practices that sustain the kind of power traditionally linked with a rapacious form of masculinity.

The workplace systems that give rise to sexual abuses are complex. In recent legal trials of media men, survivors of these men's assaults were cross-examined about why they continued to stay in sexual relationships with their assailants; why they remained in seemingly friendly communication with them; why they had "put themselves in positions" where they could be assaulted; why they never reported the incidents. But "individuals are the capillaries through which power diffuses itself through culture,"[93] and the systems of power that held victims and perpetrators of sexual assault in an ongoing abusive dynamic were entrenched and seemingly inescapable. This is because rapacious masculinity is articulated to power at individual, organizational, and societal levels. Rapacious masculinity is not an inherently male quality; rather it is an embodied construction sustained by an intersecting array of factors—an "intricate interplay of social and political power, sexual hierarchization, and embodiment."[94]

The unmuting of women by the MeToo movement, freeing them as it did to speak about their individual experiences of sexual violence, is a crucial first step in confronting male rapacity. But, as this analysis points out, rapacious masculinity is institutionally and societally engendered and supported. Individual narratives must be yoked to more macro-level processes in order for change to occur. The feminist psychologist Nicola Gavey notes that "it is within normative cultural parameters of heterosex for men to aggressively pursue sex and women to resist it."[95] But, she adds, "this particular pattern of sex is so rigidly *gendered* and ritualized it not only limits sexual agency for women, but it provides too tidy an alibi for rape."[96] It is this cultural "alibi" that allows sexual predators to continue their violations, safeguarded by institutional and social norms. Stemming the tide of sexual assault therefore calls for feminist structural analyses, solutions, and actions that revolutionize our ways of thinking about sexual violence.

Of Presidents and Pussy Grabs

Silences, and silencing, deflect attention from the reality that sexual harassment is pervasive, occurring in various contexts and cultures. Globally, an estimated 2 billion women, or 75 percent of all women, have experienced workplace sexual harassment. It is becoming clear that the framework enabling sexual assault and harassment—the overarching ethos of rape culture—is comprised of multiple levels of practices and processes. This is to say that the seemingly independent acts of individual predators within organizations are shaped by, and in turn shape, organizational cultures. Similarly, organizational cultures engage interactively with the larger social environment. These levels of practice—individual, organizational, societal—are woven into an interrelated and dynamic system and all of them operate concurrently to embed rape culture into so many aspects of social life that sexual assault and harassment have become taken-for-granted norms; they are only just beginning to be publicly recognized, challenged, and counteracted.

Rape culture's institutionalization in society is clear in the overtly rape-supportive rhetoric used by world leaders who publicly endorse sexual violence, especially against women, a trend that parallels the rise of despotic populism in many nations and regions. These men—Silvio Berlusconi of Italy, Rodrigo Duterte of the Philippines, Donald Trump of the United States, among others—are "a dangerous threat to human rights,"[97] and rape culture is endemic to their agendas, as evidenced in their unambiguous references to rape as a normal and even justifiable behavior. The perspectives, attitudes, and behaviors of political leaders matter: they shape public agendas and opinions. "People are predisposed to accept presidential leadership on public policies; the public has a demand or appetite for presidential leadership," writes the political scientist Jeffrey Cohen.[98]

Importantly, these men have a significant media presence. The impact of rape culture in the media thus occurs not just within the concrete-and-glass structures of media organizations but in the imbrication of these organizations with political power. Rape culture is in part woven into the social fabric thanks to the way it is represented and circulated via the media.

Media culture as a lightning rod for rape culture is exemplified in the now infamous *Access Hollywood* video that exposed US President Donald Trump's sexual attitudes and behaviors. While the video captured a particular incident, its repercussions bring into view the larger social and structural embedding of rape culture. The ripple effects of the tape had significant sociopolitical consequences that continue to shape contemporary life.

To recap: in 2016, Trump was a candidate in the US presidential election. Late in the campaign, the *Washington Post* released a decade-old video from an NBC entertainment news program in which Trump had been recorded, without his knowledge, in conversation with Billy Bush, the show's host.[99] On the "hot mic" recording, Trump boasted of having made a sexual advance on a female acquaintance: "I did try and fuck her. I admit it. She was married ... I moved on her like a bitch," he said;[100] he then talked freely about his views of women's sexual availability to men like him:

> You know, I'm automatically attracted to beautiful [women]—I just start kissing them. It's like a magnet. Just kiss. I don't even wait. And when you're a star, they let you do it. You can do anything. ... Grab them by the pussy. You can do anything.[101]

Once released, the video was picked up by national and international news outlets. Trump's response was dismissive: "This was locker-room banter, a private conversation that took place many years ago."[102] Trump was already a polarizing figure; the rationalization of his vulgar remarks triggered an even greater polarization among the American electorate. A discerning analysis by the media scholar Dustin Harp shows that the fallout from the video highlighted a struggle between patriarchal gender norms and pro-feminist resistance in American society.[103] Trump's supporters—male and female—latched on to the "locker room" reference, excusing his comments with a "boys will be boys" mindset that appeared to characterize the future leader of the nation as an adolescent and to show casual disregard for the problematic lack of maturity associated with that construal.

Critics of the president confronted his taped remarks from a feminist standpoint, interpreting them as a clear description of sexual assault. In addition, some men repudiated the "locker room" as a metaphor for the alleged vulgarity of male athletes, protesting that athletes as well as other men have great respect for women and would never have expressed the views that Trump did. This critique broached the possibility of alternative masculinities as a challenge to Trump's rapacious masculinity.

Harp notes that the "sexual assault" interpretation of Trump's boasts invoked "a feminist understanding of rape culture."[104] Rape culture is constituted in part through public narratives. The way in which sex is "put into discourse,"[105] to use Foucault's phrase, shapes and regulates its real-world configurations and interpretations; or, as Will Stockton puts it, "discourses of sexuality often determine what qualifies as sex in the first place."[106] In that sense, rape culture "is a complex of beliefs that encourages male sexual aggression and supports violence against women."[107]

Trump's accounts of forcibly kissing and groping women are in line with a worldview in which men have unfettered access to women's bodies and consent is assumed ("they let you do it"). Trump's attitude signals the sexual entitlement that powerful men in media and other workplaces have assumed to be a perquisite of their positions.

The media can be a source of such beliefs, but they were also the site of the public disclosure of Trump's comments on *Access Hollywood*, which happened first in the *Washington Post* and then in multiple other outlets. In many ways, the media environment provides a complex site for the enactment of rape culture. On the one hand, media images and texts can contribute to a systemic validation of rape myths and pro-rape attitudes. On the other, they can clarify the parameters and impact of rape culture and catalyze resistance and social change.

The release of the tape did not prevent Trump's 2016 election as president of the United States. Before the election, a survey found that, while some 80 percent of the US electorate was aware of the *Access Hollywood* video, Republican voters were undeterred by it: "the tape didn't change how they saw Trump at all."[108] Trump has continued to talk about women in demeaning ways, sending a powerful message that "women are disposable objects, useful for sex and childbearing but not human beings deserving of respect and dignity, let alone power."[109] Political values and voting behaviors reflect personal values,[110] so Trump's election has been a referendum on rape culture at a societal level.

These themes have played out globally as well. The Italian media mogul Silvio Berlusconi, who was elected prime minister three times between 1994 and

2011, co-opted the objectification and degradation of women as hallmarks of his governance—he even suggested renaming his political party Forza Gnocca ("Go Pussy").[111] He was renowned for hosting orgiastic bunga bunga parties with sex workers and fellow politicians, and in 2013 he was convicted of paying for sex with an underage girl at one of these blowouts (the conviction was later overturned for lack of evidence). His sexist comments to women are well documented; there is for instance an incident where he asked a young professional woman, onstage at a public event: "Do you come? How many times?"[112]

The Brazilian President Jair Bolsonaro said to a female politician: "I would not rape you, because you are not worthy of it." President Rodrigo Duterte of the Philippines told soldiers to shoot female guerilla fighters "in the vagina" because that would render them "useless."[113] His remarks drew laughter from a crowd of supporters. The Australian MP David Leyonhjelm told Greens Party Senator Sarah Hanson-Young to "stop shagging men" when she blamed rape on male aggression; now she is suing him for defamation.[114] In parliament, Kumara Welgama, the Sri Lankan transportation minister, responded to a question posed by politician Rosy Senanayake by sexually propositioning her.[115] The British Prime Minister Boris Johnson has a history of sexist comments and behaviors that include referring to women MPs as "hot totty" (British slang for sexy women) and quipping that the wives of male Tory voters would grow "bigger breasts."[116] The Mexican President Andrés Manuel López Obrador claims that violence against women is largely a fiction.[117]

The fact that these men hold influential political positions demonstrates that a misogynistic belief system can be institutionally entrenched, supported, and rewarded by the political apparatus at national levels, across many regions and contexts. These men are among the most powerful people in their countries and are part of an inner circle of decision makers whose ideologies and values determine national policies and other key principles of governance; they are held up as exemplars and voted into office by millions of admiring supporters. Their freely expressed objectifying and sexualized remarks to, and about, women contribute to the discursive construction of rape culture—and the weight of that contribution is significant, given the scope of their influence. Their public comments, disseminated via the media to audiences throughout their nations and the world, explicitly construct women as sexual objects and in many cases endorse violence towards them.

The representation of these views does not simply exhibit or reflect the corresponding ideologies, it recirculates them, articulating them to the power and position of the sources. The simplest and most straightforward way for an audience member to interpret mediatized narratives delivered by powerful men is to regard them as legitimate, even favored models of social relations. There is, then, a cultural transmission that occurs through the mediatization of misogynistic worldviews. Rape culture is embedded in the media spectacle of world leaders' misogyny and thus consecrated as an officially sanctioned and institutionally protected social phenomenon.

However, the media remain a contested terrain, where

various ideologies struggle for validation through representation. As Douglas Kellner has argued, media culture "induces individuals to conform to the established organization of society, but it also provides resources that can empower individuals against that society."[118]

Thus a spirited and widespread feminist rejection of rape culture was equally sparked by the *Access Hollywood* video. Around the globe, over 4 million people participated in Women's Marches held on January 21, 2017 to protest Trump's inauguration. An emblem of the worldwide protests was the "pussyhat," a pink handknit cap featuring ears like a cat's. The website for the Pussyhat Project explains that the hat's design "was chosen in part as a protest against vulgar comments Donald Trump made about the freedom he felt to grab women's genitals, to de-stigmatize the word 'pussy' and transform it into one of empowerment..."[119]

While the hat unquestionably referenced and talked back to Trump's comments, its meaning extended to resistant ideologies that exceeded this narrow focus. A survey of people attending the US marches revealed that they wore the hats as markers of solidarity with diverse global citizens who were "expressing disagreement with the US political climate" and were "supporters of women, LGBTQ, immigrant, and minority rights."[120] Numerous respondents "declared they were 'taking back the pussy'" and said the hat symbolized "unity, solidarity, and/or empowerment."[121] Although in recent years the hat has been criticized for excluding nonbinary and trans people as well as people of color, at the time it was a potent signifier of solidarity across identities and differences. "The pussyhat originated in liberal, white, middle-class women's choices about work and essentialist notions of gender that have not held up well to critical scrutiny," notes Ann Larabee. "And yet, somehow, the Women's March on Washington galvanized an intersectional resistance—even some men were wearing pussyhats that day—that pushed the pussyhat into a signifier of pure opposition."[122]

Despite the problematic provenance of the pussyhat itself, the *Access Hollywood* tape and its signification of rape culture played a key role in mobilizing worldwide protests not just against Trump but in support of progressive politics on a wide array of fronts.

The marches were not formally connected with the MeToo movement. But the marches, and Trump's inauguration as the 45th president of the United States, "opened the way for a watershed year of women telling the truth about our experiences," as columnist Mia Sanders put it.[123] When the marchers roared into the streets in January 2017, they powerfully embodied the expressed rejection of rape culture and of myriad other assaults on human rights and dignity. Many of the marchers had never declared themselves in this way before. Thus the Women's Marches marked a collective coming "into voice" of people who were no longer willing to suffer degradation in silence or isolation. As such, they can be thought of as a MeToo moment—a collective silence breaking, radically inclusive though led by women, and designed to challenge systemic oppression.

The marches mobilized a groundswell of intersectional activism, at least initially. In the United States, an unprecedented number of women ran for elected office in 2018, many citing the marches as their motivation and inspiration.[124] The candidacies of women of color and other people from marginalized and minoritized communities were notable. The Time's Up organization, created in 2018 and inspired by MeToo as well as by the marches, emphasizes inclusivity as it provides legal counsel and funding along with political advocacy to combat sexual harassment. Globally, too, women have continued to agitate for progressive change. For example, in Chile the feminist collective Linea Aborto Libre set up hotlines to "ensure that women have access to safe abortion information, care, medicine and back-up support when needed," in direct response to Trump's global gag rule, which stopped US aid to agencies that provided information on reproductive rights.[125] In Bolsonaro's Brazil, the group SOS Corpo–Feminist Institute for Democracy spearheads community organizing, particularly focusing on women in poverty, women of color, LGBTQ, and indigenous peoples.

But the Women's March has had its share of controversy as well, including allegations of racism, anti-Semitism, and insensitivity to the realities of regional politics. In fact a splinter group called March On has emerged, and it is more focused on inclusivity and local organizing in "right-to-work" states in the United States, for example.[126] In the wake of the critiques, the Women's March diversified its board so as to include Jewish women and rebranded the organization "a space for all women"; yet the organization is still widely perceived by African American and other women of color as an exclusionary white space, insensitive to issues that affect more marginalized communities.[127]

Two decades earlier, the writer Louise Armstrong worried that "breaking the silence [had] come to be an end in itself,"[128] dysfunctionally self-absorbed rather than leading to action and social change. The period after the first march belied that concern by offering evidence of real-world reforms, if not revolution. Yet three years later the momentum has dwindled. The Women's March organization has not yet fulfilled its promise of turning into an engine for a feminist paradigm shift. Nonetheless, the 2020 march in Washington, DC featured the Chilean feminist collective Las Tesis and its anthem, "Un violador en tu camino" ("A rapist in your path"), which keeps the focus on rape culture, a concept the marches helped to bring to the forefront of public consciousness.

The examples above demonstrate how certain modes of privileged masculinity exploit power and position at national and even global levels, in terms of sexual entitlement and aggression. The basic tenets of the institutionalization of rape culture apply across organizational contexts, political configurations, geographic regions, and cultures.

Against this juggernaut, resistant consciousness-raising—through marches, community organizing, online discussions, and the rallying cry of "MeToo"—has awakened realizations, kindled political commitments, and started to forge solidarities across differences. This trajectory portends systemic change. Criticisms of, and challenges to, the movement are widening its scope, bringing an intersectional feminist agenda into clearer focus.

2
Representation

E-race-ures

TIME magazine's 2017 Person of the Year was awarded to "the silence breakers." The magazine cover featured a diverse array of women, wearing somber black and looking directly into the camera: the actor Ashley Judd, the singer Taylor Swift, the former Uber engineer Susan Fowler, the corporate lobbyist Adama Iwu, and the pseudonymous farm worker Isabel Pascual. To the right of the photograph, the arm of a faceless woman was identified as "Anonymous," a hospital worker fearful of consequences after she reported her sexual harassment. The cover line read: "The silence breakers: The voices that launched a movement."

The cover appeared to offer a powerful pro-feminist statement of solidarity and progress. But conspicuously absent from the cover image was Tarana Burke, the MeToo movement's founder.

The cover's emancipatory overtones belied a form of racialized effacement. While the diversity of the movement was showcased through the inclusion of women of different racial identities and job descriptions on the cover image, the black woman who had initiated it was pointedly erased. Social movement leaders have been selected as *TIME*'s Person of the Year in the past: Mahatma Gandhi in 1930, Martin Luther King Jr. in 1963, Lech Walesa in 1981. No women of color have ever earned this recognition, and *TIME*'s decision not to recognize Burke as the founder and catalyzer of the MeToo movement raises important questions about the leadership of women of color and, perhaps even more importantly, about the politics of invisibility: it is the failure to *see* and to honor the work being done in marginalized communities and unseen spaces. This is work that impels and nourishes the "new" feminist activism against rape culture, and its intentional intersectionality extends far beyond the activism of cisgender women.

Burke has repeatedly emphasized that the movement is not about her, but about survivors. Yet her absence from the cover photograph is worth thinking about. Her dauntless struggles to call attention to sexual violence express an activist consciousness that recognized, long before it was trendy, the power of speaking and sharing truths. The cover purported to celebrate those who had "launched the movement," but it deliberately left out the African American woman who actually *had* launched it.

Burke's activism built upon a long history of African American women's efforts to break deep silences around sexual violence. As far back as two centuries ago, despite having no legal status as persons or citizens, enslaved black women in the Americas strove to publicly expose and decry their sexual violations at the hands of white slave owners. "Their campaigns for sexual justice took many forms, from written protest to violent resistance," writes the historian Crystal Feimster.[1] The writings of the slave Mary Prince, published in 1831, denounced the savage sexualized beatings she endured from the married white couple who owned her; Harriet Jacobs's *Incidents in the Life of a Slave Girl* (1861) "highlighted her master's sexual power over her in ways that revealed her resistance";[2] and the 1855 trial of a teenage slave named Celia, who killed her white master after years of enduring rape at his hands, launched a legal debate over whether black women could be recognized as rape victims.[3] The answer turned out to be "no," and Celia was executed for murder. Nonetheless, notes Feimster, "Celia had succeeded in making visible black women's campaigns for human dignity and sexual justice."[4] A legacy of resistance was upheld by generations of black slave women who "were beaten and raped, but never subdued."[5]

Toward the end of the nineteenth century, the abolitionist writer and speaker Ida B. Wells published the pamphlet *Southern Horrors*, a manifesto against the wanton and barbaric lynchings of black men for alleged rapes of white women—claims that were usually fraudulent and, as she argued, served as convenient cover for white men's sexual assaults of black women.[6] Black women in the United States had little recourse against sexual assault, especially when the perpetrators were white, until legislation during the postwar Reconstruction enabled them to file a smattering of successful claims against rapists. Those gains were short-lived: the imposition of segregationist Jim Crow laws toward the turn of the century effectively nullified any progress that had been made. Yet African American women persevered in the battle against sexual violence. The civil rights leader Rosa Parks was "an antirape activist long before she became the patron saint of the bus boycott."[7] "Throughout the twentieth century," writes the historian Danielle McGuire, "black women persisted in telling their stories, frequently cited in local and national NAACP reports. Their testimonies spilled out in letters to the Justice Department and appeared on the front pages of the nation's leading black newspapers. Black women regularly denounced their sexual misuse."[8]

Tarana Burke stands as a key intercept on this powerful trajectory of resistance to rape. She is a pivotal figure, a living link between the future of intersectional anti-rape solidarity and the deep roots of African American women's history of unflagging activism against sexual violence. Her exclusion from the Person of the Year cover image ignored both the originative significance of her work and an associated legacy of powerful protest. As the film director Melissa V. Murray observed, "the outrage over Tarana's absence on the cover isn't about who gets credit for the hashtag—it's about the marginalization of black women in movements that we've started."[9]

Tarana Burke's absence speaks also to the muting of other histories and experiences of sexual violence and resistance. Burke herself has been vocal about the scope of this absence: "The women of color, trans women, queer people—our stories get pushed aside and our pain is never prioritized. We don't talk about indigenous women. Their stories go untold."[10] For people whose communities have been scarred by centuries of sexual violence, #MeToo carries raw reminders of repression and derogation that continue today.

The absence to consider, then, is not simply that of Tarana Burke herself. Rather it is made up of the missing histories of resistance to sexual violence that the *TIME* cover image still silenced in its tribute to "silence breakers." An absence is not a null category. Absences are meaningful: they testify to deletions; they contain multitudes of erasures and omissions. It would be a serious error to gloss over an absence, leaving it unremarked. Indeed, *TIME*'s editors failed to notice this absence. But women of color saw it immediately, as soon as the Person of the Year issue hit newsstands. To see the invisible is a specific type of vision—a superpower held by the powerless. It is precisely this vision that mobilizes social justice activism.

What does this absence reveal to those who can see it? First, the long view—not only the history of African American women's resistance to sexual violence, but an intertwined history of other women of color who have also fought hard against it. For these women, resistance to sexual violence "cannot be understood outside of colonialism and today's ongoing racism and genocide," writes the feminist scholar Sherene Rezack. "When women from marginalized communities speak out against sexual violence, we are naming something infinitely broader than what men do to women within our communities …"[11] So the harrowingly high rates of sexual violence against American Indian and Alaskan Native women today are traceable to the European conquest of the Americas. "[R]ape in the lives of Native women is not an epidemic of recent, mysterious origin," notes the legal scholar Sarah Deer. "Instead, rape is a fundamental result of colonialism, a history of violence reaching back centuries. … Native American women experience the trauma of rape as an enduring violence that spans generations."[12] The history of subjugation of people of color—indigenous peoples, enslaved peoples, displaced peoples, minoritized peoples—is also a history of sexual violence against them. Women of color were most often raped by colonizers and slavers, but people of color of all genders experienced sexual brutality at the hands of these same people and through their policies. Racism has been, and still is, a tactic used to justify invasions and to advance nation building: the violability of a land is tantamount to the violability of its inhabitants' bodies, in the colonizer's view. Unclaimed land is "virgin" territory: the metaphor is sexual.

In a contemporary manifestation of colonial aggression, the construction of oil pipelines in the Great Lakes and Great Plains regions of the United States is precipitating a rise in sexual assaults against, and increased sex trafficking of, American Indian women.[13] Extractive industries, such as oil and gas drilling, attract a labor force made up of males who live in "man camps" on Native lands, and the presence of transient men is a direct cause of escalation in the rates of sexual violence against Native women.[14] Yet throughout this history "strength and survival are also critical components of the story of violence and First Nations women."[15] Before the European invasion, women held powerful roles in Native societies, and sexual violence was virtually unknown. Deer points out that "European settlers were fascinated and sometimes horrified by the sexual autonomy of Native women."[16] The imposition of European patriarchal mores robbed Native women of their status and agency and subjected them to intense sexual violations perpetrated by the European settlers. But, from colonial times onward, Native women have engaged in various forms of refusal, strategic as well as physical. In 1495, the Spanish conquistador Michele de Cuneo wrote of his rape of a "Carib" woman who "was unwilling for me to do so [i.e. have sex with her], and treated me with her nails in such wise that I would have preferred never to have begun."[17] (He nonetheless beat her into submission with a rope and sexually assaulted her.) Throughout the history of American colonization, despite continual violations of every kind, "Native American women advocated for political and economic self-sufficiency for themselves and their communities."[18] In the twentieth century, groups such as WARN (Women of All Red Nations) and the Indian Law Resource Center began to engage deeply in organized resistance on a range of women's issues, including sexual assault, and leaders such as Tillie Black Bear and Lenora Hootch fought for survivors' rights. These activists were instrumental in the passage of the first Violence Against Women Act, laying the groundwork for indigenous anti-rape and anti-violence movements that are growing and active on multiple fronts today, for example the White Buffalo Calf Women's Society, Mending the Sacred Hoop, and MMIW (Missing and Murdered Indigenous Women). This history is unmentioned—silenced—in *TIME*'s "silence breakers" tribute.

The same goes for other absent histories of resistance to sexual violence. Asian Pacific Islander (API) women have experienced and resisted racist and colonial sexual violence, both within the United States and in various regions of Asia and the Pacific during American military operations. The "taming" of the American West and the development of transnational railroad systems catalyzed the first surge of Asian immigration to the United States in the late nineteenth and twentieth centuries, when men from China, Japan, Korea, and the Philippines were recruited to perform backbreaking work on plantations and construction sites. But a dramatic gender imbalance resulted when Chinese women were banned from immigrating. As a consequence of these structural conditions, the Asian (particularly Chinese) women who entered the country were often forced into prostitution. "[T]he large number of young Chinese girls and women who were forced to work as prostitutes lived lives of degradation, illness, and poverty, and many were parts of organized tongs"[19]—what we would call sex-trafficking rings today. These women were sexually assaulted and abused, stigmatized, and penalized. And yet they found ways to escape and resist sexual servitude and violence by running away, by marrying Asian men, by seeking help from white allies, or even through "insanity or suicide."[20] Over the years, shifts in immigration policies and various US military interventions overseas changed the contours of the API–American population; like other immigrant histories, theirs is marked by sexual and other forms of violence—and resistance to it. Gina Marie Weaver's account of the brutal rapes of Vietnamese women by American GIs during the mid-twentieth century conflict in Southeast Asia describes the "strength and heroism" with which many women fought against and survived this violence. Their sexual torture at the hands of US soldiers was extreme: at the 1967 International War Crimes Tribunal, one woman's testimony described a soldier who "stripped her, tied her arms, and thrust his hand into her vagina until blood came and she cried out in pain"; another woman "died after a broken bottle was inserted into her vagina."[21] Weaver notes that, by bearing witness to their own rape, women are committed to "the formation of a public that will actively seek to resolve the continuing plight of sufferers."[22] As for the United States itself, as early as 1978 Nilda Rimonte, a Filipina American, established the Center for the Pacific–Asian Family in Los Angeles, to provide resources for battered and sexually abused Asian American women.[23] Her legacy is far-reaching: today various pan-Asian activist organizations support survivors of rape and other forms of sexual assault and abuse. The need for services continues to outstrip their availability, and feminist activism perseveres in this area. Rimonte and API feminism were also absent from *TIME*'s record of resistance.

The *TIME* cover did feature a Latina woman, dubbed Isabel Pascual—a pseudonym. An agricultural worker, she was sexually harassed, stalked, and threatened with violence by a male perpetrator. Her story is far from being an isolated case. "Hundreds and thousands of women and girls in the United States today work in fields, packing houses, and other agricultural workplaces where they face a real and significant risk of sexual violence and sexual harassment," states a recent report from Human Rights Watch.[24] Because many of these women are undocumented, speak little or no English, and are in economically precarious positions, they almost never report the assaults, which are commonly committed by "foremen, supervisors, farm labor contractors, company owners and anyone else who has the power to hire and fire workers as well as confer certain benefits, such as better hours or permission to take breaks."[25] Any pushback from the women results in harsh penalties, which encompass joblessness, homelessness, detention, and deportation. Legal representation is generally unavailable, especially to women without visas. Despite all this, women farmworkers have been organizing against sexual violence for decades. An example is the Alianza Nacional de Campesinas, which represents the 700,000 women farmworkers in the United States. Alianza is now well known for writing an open letter to the Hollywood actors who had launched #MeToo on Twitter, catalyzing the creation of the Time's Up legal fund that defends survivors of sexual harassment and abuse, "especially low-income women and people of color."[26] And yet *TIME*'s "silence breakers" cover and story did not recognize the work of Mily Treviño-Saucedo and Mónica Ramírez, who co-founded the Alianza after years of organizing farmworkers and advocating against sexual violence. Again, the sustained leadership of women of color as pathbreakers in the fight against rape and workplace sexual abuses was not part of *TIME*'s story.

Intersectional issues of gender and sexuality haunt Tarana Burke's absence from the *TIME* cover in complicated ways. While the experiences of women of color were quickly recuperated in the #MeToo discourse, the movement has been hegemonically heterosexual.

Various forms of sexual violence against LGBTQ people have only recently begun to be recognized as crucial social issues. The feminist scholar Ann Russo has pointed out that today "lesbians and bisexual women face denial and passivity by the feminist antiviolence movement" and "have few resources to find support and advocacy."[27] Similarly, trans activism has for decades tackled police brutality, the high rate of murder of trans people, and a range of political and legal issues, but sexual violence is just now emerging as an area of focus. As a trans activist, the actor Laverne Cox has stressed the intersectionality of sexual assault, recognizing the impact of race, class, and gender and emphasizing that sexual violence cuts across categories of identity with varying impacts and consequences; as she points out, "it's not just women who are experiencing sexual assault."[28]

TIME's "silence breakers" issue erases the fact that resistance is a hallmark in the evolution of the rights of sexually marginalized, gender-nonconforming, and trans people. As long ago as in the 1950s, organizations such as the Mattachine Society and the Daughters of Bilitis challenged violence against gay and lesbian people, as did several activist groups that followed, for example the Gay Liberation Front. The Stonewall Riots of 1969 are, of course, the best-known instance of LGBTQ resistance to harassment; they have been described as "the first acts of gay and lesbian resistance ever."[29] The Compton's Cafeteria Riot of 1966 was another early example of fighting against police harassment, this time by trans activists in San Francisco.[30] In the 1970s, lesbian feminists led the development of "projects that addressed sexual health, reproductive freedom, and violence against women";[31] the Ohio group Women Against Rape is one example. "That lesbian women were central in the antirape movement undoubtedly shaped the feminist analysis of rape as an act representing one end of the continuum of … 'heterosex,'"[32] write the feminist scholars Verta Taylor and Leila J. Rupp. Recently, lesbian and trans activists were early supporters of Aishah Shahidah Simmons's anti-rape documentary "NO!"

When we turn to sexual violence against people with disabilities, these complexities are amplified. For men and women with disabilities, the rates of serious violent crimes, including rape, are more than twice as high as for nondisabled people; and they are higher still for all people of color with disabilities.[33] National Public Radio reports that "people with intellectual disabilities are sexually assaulted at more than seven times the rate of people without disabilities."[34] This issue gained national attention in 1989, when a teenager with intellectual disabilities was brutally gang-raped by four wealthy young white men in Glenn Ridge, New Jersey—forced by her assailants to perform oral sex on them and then penetrated with a baseball bat and a broomstick. As with LGBTQ people, resources for sexual violence survivors with disabilities are scarce; such survivors are even "screened out from rape crisis centers or feel unwelcomed when they do show up."[35] Despite this systemic neglect, the disability rights movement has engaged in sustained advocacy and activism against sexual violence. In 2018 the National Council on Disability issued a damning report, "Not on the Radar," which demonstrated that, despite the alarmingly high incidence of sexual violence against them, college students with disabilities are completely overlooked by campus sexual assault services, as well as by funding agencies. The report led to the introduction in 2019 of the US Senate Bill 984, which adds services for people with disabilities to earlier legislation on higher education; the bill is pending. In the wake of #MeToo, the organizations Rooted in Rights and the Disability Visibility Project launched a Twitter conversation where people with disabilities could share stories of sexual assault and abuse. The responses poured in at #DisabilityToo. A woman described reporting a stalker, only to be told: "Impossible. Why would he stalk you?"[36] Another revealed that "[t]he wheelchair attendant at an airport groped me when we were alone in an elevator."[37] Repeated and sustained sexual abuse was disclosed by people of all genders and sexualities. "I think the purpose of all these stories is to really motivate us and politicize us, and … to think about the work ahead. We all have the power to do something. And I think the stories are that spark," reflected the writer and organizer Alice Wong, who has spent decades working for disability rights.[38]

Men with disabilities experience sexual violence at

much higher rates than nondisabled men. But nondisabled men are sexually victimized, too. Overall, the experiences of male survivors are perhaps the most hidden and discounted of all MeToo stories. This may be because men are overwhelmingly the perpetrators of sexual assaults, and women are overwhelmingly the victim-survivors, so the dominant dynamic is heterosexual. Yet same-sex violence happens among men, and men are sometimes violated by women; these experiences are seldom addressed in public discourse. For men, the difficulty of reporting sexual violence and seeking help is tremendous, heightened as it is by social mores and rape myths that disavow the reality of their experiences. This difficulty is further complicated by whether they are trans, cis, gay, or straight, as well as by race, class, nation, ability, and other aspects of their identities and social locations.

The issue is still bound up in shame and secrecy for many men. Most men are raped by other men,[39] though other forms of sexual violence and abuse are increasingly found to involve female perpetrators. Like sexual assault on people of all genders, male sexual victimization is underreported, even more so than victimization among women.[40] The social barriers to reporting carry enormous weight. Men are culturally positioned as sexual aggressors; masculine identity is tied to sexual dominance, and victimization is therefore interpreted as a failure of masculinity. Same-sex victimization also carries overtones of homosexuality, which, again, is read negatively in a heteronormative society: "for gay and bisexual male survivors, negative attitudes about homosexuality may construct the notion that this form of violence is normal or deserved."[41] Rape myths underpin men's failure to report; such myths include the notion that only women can be raped, the notion that men are unrapable because they should be able to defend themselves against attacks, or the notion that men always enjoy sex or are not harmed by nonconsensual sex. (The actor Terry Crews, mentioned in the *TIME* story, faced accusations along such lines after he reported being sexually assaulted.) And indeed, because of these myths, authorities are less likely to believe men's reports of assault and services are less available for men. Still, consciousness is starting to shift as men are telling their stories: stories of being raped while in military service, or on photo shoots as male models, or by their partners. More than 150 former wrestlers at Ohio State University testified about being sexually abused by a team physician, Dr. Richard Strauss. The external investigation into the abuse noted that "the student-athletes were generally expected to be 'the manliest of men,'"[42] a stereotype that prevented them from disclosing the assaults and undermined their claims when they did report. "I have mental health issues due to the rape I was subjected to," writes a man on the #MeTooMen Twitter feed. "Not ashamed of it one bit but I will not let it define me. The fight is Real."[43]

The fight *is* real. The #MeToo rebellion began in the United States as a cause of wealthy white women, but rapidly morphed into a broad-based social movement that embraced women of color, women from various class backgrounds, women of different sexual orientations, women with disabilities, and eventually people of all genders, sexualities, abilities, and embodied subjectivities. It has global reach as well. The MeToo movement "has now reached nearly every region of the world; the phrase itself, and the viral hashtag #MeToo, is in regular rotation in more than 85 nations."[44]

Tarana Burke's absence as a "silence breaker" is connected to the global scope of the movement, also absent from *TIME*'s cover or coverage of Person of the Year. There are intersections and strong bonds among Burke's work, the work of other women of color, the work of LGBQ and trans people, and the work of women and others in places such as Indonesia, France, Egypt, and Mexico, where anti-rape activism pre-dated the hashtag.

Women's resistance, especially to injustices created by systems of patriarchal power, is too often trivialized or dismissed as a "moral panic about racial, sexual and gender identity."[45] The *TIME* cover was a clear visual countercharge to those dismissals, appropriately celebrating women's key role in making sexual harassment, assault, and abuse paramount issues in 2017. Yet the conspicuous absence of the black woman who actually launched the MeToo movement called forth other silences, the hidden histories of sexual assault and resistance that have unfolded over centuries in spaces and places unseen and unheralded, spaces and places that mark the intersections of gender, race, nation, class, disability, and sexuality with sexual violence.

Thinking of absence in this way reveals the power of an unfilled space. An absence of this sort is not a void; it is not empty. Rather it is a fertile place, gravid with meaning. "A structuring absence," explains the media scholar Richard Dyer,

> refers to an issue, or even a set of facts or an argument, that a text cannot ignore, but which it deliberately skirts round or otherwise avoids, thus creating the biggest "holes" in the text, fatally, revealingly misshaping the organic whole assembled with such craft.[46]

In reflecting upon *TIME*'s 2017 "Person of the Year" cover image, identifying a significant absence draws attention to the problems with the "organic whole," which isn't actually whole because of the omissions. Recognizing and calling out a structuring absence requires an "active reading" of images like this one, in order "to make them say what they have to say *within* what they leave unsaid, to reveal their constituent lacks."[47] Seeing an absence in this way is indeed a revelation, as well as a form of social justice activism that by itself breaks silences around rape culture.

The Naked and the Damned

In 2014, when a former lover uploaded nude photographs and a sex tape of the Ugandan pop singer Desire Luzinda to social media, the images went viral and all hell broke loose. Like other victims of so-called "revenge porn," Luzinda was mercilessly denigrated, humiliated, and harassed. She was also threatened with criminal prosecution under Uganda's harsh Anti-Pornography Act: Ugandan Minister of Integrity and Ethics Simon Lokodo set the police on her, insisting that "she should be locked up and isolated."[48] Confronted with public condemnation, Luzinda apologized for her apparent transgression, expressing remorse for "her folly in agreeing to being photographed or filmed in a state of undress"[49]—even though she had never consented to the public distribution of the images or of the video. While Luzinda took the blame for these violations, the man who had actually taken and uploaded the pictures, Franklin Emuobor Ebenhron, fled the country and, to date, has faced no penalties for his actions.

Luzinda is, of course, not alone: for millions of women worldwide, nudity and sex have taken on increasingly dangerous and distressing dimensions in the virtual media environment, where rape culture has mutated into new forms. Not only is revenge porn a global scourge, but cyberstalking, illegal sexual surveillance, nonconsensual sexting, online sexual harassment, and other crimes are fueling a pro-rape environment. Online communities of "incels" (involuntary celibates) engage in fantasies of sexual violence against women and these fantasies have erupted into real-world attacks, particularly mass shootings in the United States.[50] The epidemic of violence against women "is thriving in the petri dish of social media," as the journalists Catherine Buni and Soraya Chemaly have observed.[51] Women and children are overwhelmingly the victims of sexual cybercrimes,[52] though men and trans people are sometimes targeted too.

Sexual cybercrimes exploit victims' sexuality and bodies to terrorize and torment them. As in physical rape, sex becomes a weapon, and nudity is weaponized as well. The consequences for survivors and victims are serious: they can face loss of employment, psychological trauma, the destruction of friendships and family relationships, blackmail, physical violence, even death through murder or suicide. In these ways, sexual cyber crimes are part of an apparatus of silencing. "Silencing," notes the legal scholar Danielle Keats Citron, "is what many harassers are after."[53] Online threats of rape and sexual violence have become normalized as silencing mechanisms, especially against women.[54] Victims are driven out of workplaces, virtual and real communities, and family settings; they are shamed, discredited, intimidated, and—one way or another—expunged. Desire Luzinda went into hiding;[55] PhD student Holly Jacobs changed her name and relocated;[56] teenagers Amanda Todd and Tyler Clementi committed suicide.[57] They all took the fall for their online persecution and, in different ways, they silenced themselves.

*

Naked bodies can be many things, including beautiful. (They can also be not beautiful, and both beauty and non-beauty are in the eye of the beholder.) Indeed, all kinds of bodies have been depicted by painters and poets, sculptors, photographers, filmmakers: the nude self-portraits of the photographer Laura Aguilar and the painter Egon Schiele, the women's bodies in the films of Leyla Bouzid, the Fijian men's bodies in the prints of Torika Bolatagici, the gay male bodies in the photography of Ajamu X are examples of the range of nude representation in art and in the media.

And yet, despite these varied visions, we have been taught in contemporary western culture that "a nude" designates a sexualized female body. This nude female body resonates most with a specifically heterosexual pornographic vision of female sexuality, stark naked and displayed for men's masturbatory fantasies. The woman here is a sexual turn-on and come-on: her body conveys an invitation to male voyeurism as well as a fantasy of sexual contact. Her nudity is intended for straight male arousal; through that framing, her consent to sex is presumed. She may participate willingly in this visual economy; she may find power or pleasure in self-sexualization; and, of course, none of that actually means that she has forsaken the right to consent to sexual contact. But this is tricky terrain, as, from the perspective of the male viewer, her nudity is explicitly programmed for his sexual release. This is the essence of the problematic "male gaze." Even so-called softcore pornography of this sort contributes to a sexual script that designates woman as a compliant quarry for heterosexual male desire. Her nudity is meant to cause *his* erection, *his* ejaculation—and she is presumptively delighted by that; her desire and pleasure are supposed to stem only from this dynamic. This conceit makes it hardly surprising that some 80 percent of porn users are straight men.[58]

To contemplate this setup is to recognize that bodies are more than biological facts—they have social meanings. Philosophers speak of the "lived body," and some even consider bodies to be wholly socially constructed. "The body is in no sense naturally or innately psychical, sexual, or sexed," writes the philosopher Elizabeth Grosz. "It is indeterminate and indeterminable outside its social constitution as a body of a particular type."[59] The body unclothed is particularly freighted. In the

Judeo-Christian tradition, the story of Adam and Eve yokes nudity to "original sin" and shame, the fall from grace. In line with this view, nudity in western culture has historically been used to demean and degrade. Slaves were stripped when sold at auction; the "Hottentot Venus" Saartjie (Sarah) Baartman was displayed naked, in a cage, for the enjoyment of dressed Victorian spectators; women's suffrage protestors were stripped naked and tortured at the Occoquan Work House in 1917; Jewish prisoners were stripped in Hitler's concentration camps; Abu Ghraib detainees were stripped during the Iraq War; incarcerated people are still strip-searched in US prisons. Forcible nudity is a form of humiliation, an act of subjugation, an expression of dominance, bound up with race, class, nation, gender, and sex and their intersections. Sexual overtones are at play, and in all these instances the naked person is unequivocally among the damned. Even voluntary nudity is looked at askance: many municipal codes ban public nudity as an offense and a scandal. People have nightmares about appearing naked in public places, and these dreams are deemed by psychologists to have roots in trauma. Nudity in most societies is either tainted or taboo.

But the nudity of women is more complicated than that, especially as it is represented for the public gaze. In a well-known essay, the art historian John Berger points out that nudes in classical European paintings are almost always female, and they are on display for the erotic pleasure of clothed male spectators. Nude women, he writes, are depicted "to feed [a male] appetite, not to have any of their own."[60] Women's nude bodies are not simply biological facts; they have long been coded as intended for heterosexual arousal. Even now, there is an insistent heteronormativity at work in representations of women's nudity. Mainstream American media, in particular, "characterize women's bodies as sexual objects built for male pleasure."[61] The media are pervaded by images of nude and semi-nude women, all presented erotically, for the benefit of a presumptive straight male viewer. Even in media targeted at female audiences, an implied heterosexual male spectator haunts the imagery. Although of course there are spectators who are women, trans, nonbinary, and gender-nonconforming, most mainstream media imagery is insistently geared to a heterosexual dynamic between a female object and a male viewer. The film critic Mary Ann Doane observed: "The fetishistic representation of the nude female body, fully in view, insures a masculinisation of the spectatorial position."[62] Media images construct "a woman who desires to be desired by men," a "sexually irresistible" subject,[63] inviting women to identify with her, and at the same time encouraging women as well as men—indeed everyone—to gaze at her body with desire. Her primary role is as object of desire.

Women's nudity is a routine feature in various media genres, from advertising to pornography to social networking sites. In mainstream film and television, full frontal nudity is frequent and highly gendered: female actors are routinely shown fully undressed, often with their genitalia revealed, while male actors almost never are. "[F]emale nudity is considered commonplace (reflecting the normalization of women as sexual objects)," writes the film scholar Chloé Nurik. "However, few films show full frontal male nudity, and those that do often receive harsh ratings along with a special designation marking the presence of 'male nudity.'"[64] Male genitalia, bare male bodies, are somehow sacred, to be protected from public appraisal. Nurik points out, too, that films are not allowed to represent women's self-directed sexual pleasure, as to do so would "grant subjectivity, agency, and personhood to female characters, thereby challenging hegemonic views of women and upending the male gaze."[65] As a corollary, she notes that cinematic representations of violence against women are far more acceptable than representations of women's sexual agency, and cites the film critic Mary Ann Johansen's observation that "watching a woman being murdered is less objectionable than watching a woman have an orgasm."[66]

It is interesting to consider these trends in light of the overall blurring of mainstream media and pornography, a merger that has been intensifying in recent years. Just like the mainstream media, pornography, too, features women who are fully nude more often than it does men; and in most pornography women are victims of violence. These patterns hold true over all genres of porn, including porn produced "for women,"[67] just as they do in mainstream media.

The interconnection of women's nudity, women's sexuality, and women's vulnerability to violence is a complex issue. Nudity does not, per se, invite violence. It's obvious that, in rational terms, nudity and sexual violence are not necessarily correlated. But, historically and culturally, they have been; and today they are, in most porn as well as in the media. Women are shown naked in porn more often than men, and a growing body of empirical research demonstrates that violence against women is increasing in pornography. Almost 90 percent of popular porn videos depict male physical aggression against women;[68] similar patterns are found on adult internet websites.[69] There are, of course, arguments for transgressive forms of sexual representation that offer alternatives to the objectification of the nude female body for the male gaze; these alternative media affirm sexualities that differ from hetero norms and engage diverse audiences, and are often developed by media creators from underrepresented communities. Such models may have progressive potential, but they remain a small segment of the porn and media market and are still eclipsed by the dominant heterosexuality and its ideologies of gender, which also infuse other forms of representation.

The art historian Beth Eck points out that "an image's *context* has a profound effect on one's interpretation of the nude."[70] So, in the context of heterosexual pornography that routinely emphasizes and propagates violence against women, female nudity operates as a sign of willing submission. Although porn, unlike the mainstream media, makes women's orgasms visible, these orgasms often occur as a result of violence or coercion. And even in the absence of violence, across media genres, nudity usually marks the woman as an object of male sexual desire rather than as the active subject of her own desires. Her desire is to *be desired* by men.

This is a role that sustains a rape culture.

Revenge porn and other forms of online image-based sexual violence weave these strands of nude representation together by using (and abusing) women's nudity as a form of pornographic violence, a means of silencing and humiliating women. This process is premised on equating nudity with male sexual dominance, which translates as violence. And it is a premise that has the weight of culture behind it.

It is possible to argue that pornography and media images are fantasies, and that the fiction of violence against women is not necessarily correlated with real-world rape. But, I would argue, it is correlated with rape culture, which is a system of beliefs that sustains the presumption of women's consent to sex and in which "violence is seen as sexy and sexuality as violent,"[71] violence against women is the norm rather than an atrocity, and male sexual dominance over women is entrenched through representation. In the realm of online sexual abuse and harassment, women's nudity is deployed violently and women's sexualized bodies are revealed and circulated as objects of male brutality. The imagery has serious real-world consequences for women, including the incidence of actual rape, battery, and murder.

Of course, neither nudity nor sex is tantamount to violence. It is the *mode* of representation and the gendered ideologies underpinning them that assert this connection. Yet this mode of representation, in most societies, is normalized: women's nudity is coded as sexual, and therefore shameful, while men's is hidden from view.[72] Representation matters. The media offer us role models and archetypes, norms and ideals, guardrails for navigating our lives. As Citron points out, "[l]ife online bleeds into life offline and vice versa,"[73] and this is true of all forms of media in our media-saturated environment. If rape culture suffuses media culture, dismissing it as nothing more than fantasy is a dangerous dodge.

*

Both nudity and sex are sites of pleasure, but they are also fraught with danger, as both can be weaponized to create a pro-rape environment. Recognizing this, women are combating these representational politics. In the new media environment, they are finding ways to confront, politicize, and resist these image-based assaults, in much the same way in which they have exposed and challenged "real-life" rape through feminist activism, including hashtag activism. Legal recourse is still largely inadequate and unavailable to victim-survivors, who are often counseled to disengage from public participation and online activity as a way to stop the harassment—in other words, they are silenced by the criminal justice system, which perforce aligns with the assailants.

Because of this, online spaces of resistance such as the Hollaback movement, #MeToo, and other anti-rape hashtags, along with the critical witnessing of feminist artists such as Anna Gensler, have created communities of sexual assault survivors who are naming and challenging online image-based sexual violence as well as real-world sexual violence, recognizing the commingling of these practices. The millions of people, mostly women, who participate in these spaces find "community, solidarity and support" there; these online sites and social media networks are also crucial for consciousness-raising, as participants learn to recognize and call out sexual abuse and harassment, which tend to be normalized and discounted in everyday life.[74] These resistant online practices and spaces are counteractions to the silencing function of rape culture. Their very existence "problematizes a rape culture that requires silence in order for it to flourish."[75]

Online activism of this sort is necessarily fraught with difficulties: these forms of activism generate a harsh backlash, usually from men, and they are constantly questioned with respect to their inclusivity and diversity along lines of race, class, gender identity, and sexual orientation. Considering these fallibilities, Tarana Burke's trailblazing and deeply humane work offers the philosophical and ethical grounding for this global resistance movement. When Burke started the MeToo movement, her focus was on girls and women in communities of color, communities where the prevalence of sexual violence was unstated and unaddressed. "Nobody was speaking healing into our community," she has said. "How can we heal something that we can't name?"[76] In her early work with pre-teen and teen girls, she concentrated on helping them to identify sexual violation as the source of their physical and psychic pain, to talk about their experiences of sexual abuse and assault in order to build solidarity, and to find the resources that would support their healing and recovery. Online communities of resistance are engaging in much of the same kind of work at a broader level.

Yet there is widespread skepticism about their impact

on stopping sexual violence. It is worth asking whether online activism is simply performative, an easy mode of slacktivism that doesn't translate into political action and social change. In fact the burgeoning scholarship on feminist anti-rape activism online indicates otherwise. Not only are these modes of resistance creating solidarities among survivors of sexual violence and breaking silences around experiences of sexual assault, they are also supporting survivors in reclaiming a sense of agency, affording them strategies and resources for dealing with sexual violence in their lives, and mobilizing real-world changes in policy and practice. Rosemary Clark-Parsons differentiates consumer-driven, purely representational "economies of visibility" from a "politics of visibility" that translates individual experiences into collective action.[77] Online activism and the breaking of silences around sexual violence catalyze feminist anti-rape activism. The challenge now is to take up this work in increasingly and intentionally inclusive ways.

Reporting and Rape Culture

Over the past decade, journalists have been on the frontline of tackling rape culture, and their reportorial forays have earned high praise. Pulitzer Prizes went to *Boston Globe*'s storied "Spotlight" team, for its exposé of Catholic priests' widespread sexual abuse of young children as well as of the church's deliberate cover-ups of the crimes; to the *Indianapolis Star* for investigating Dr. Larry Nassar, the serial sexual abuser, and his long history of molesting young athletes; and to the *New*

Yorker magazine and the *New York Times* for a series of stories about the serial rapist and movie mogul Harvey Weinstein. The PBS miniseries The Loudest Voice, based on the New York magazine journalist Gabriel Sherman's reporting on Roger Ailes's sexual harassment of women at Fox News, was a 2020 Golden Globe nominee. Julie K. Brown of the *Miami Herald* received high honors, including a Polk Award, for her 2018 series about a child sex trafficking ring run by the financier Jeffrey Epstein.

These journalistic investigations raised a new level of public awareness of the prevalence of rape and its embeddedness in our most respected social institutions—the Catholic Church, the Olympic Games, Hollywood, and the criminal justice system. Many of these stories were bolstered by the #MeToo/MeToo movement. Regarding the Epstein debacle, the attorney Jane Manning observed, "It's not that the girls didn't come forward years ago. The victims did come forward years ago. What's making a difference now is the brave survivors who have spoken out as part of the #MeToo movement and the advocates and journalists who have stood with them."[78] The Nassar case unfolded "amid a larger outpouring of stories about sexual assault and harassment in all arenas, from Hollywood to hotel rooms—and the people in power negligent or complicit in protecting those perpetrators."[79] The high-profile journalistic investigations indicated that the MeToo moment had emboldened a powerful ally: the press.

These trends seem to signal a promising shift in journalistic coverage of sexual violence, but there is no magic wand. Recently the feminist writer and activist

Jessica Valenti noted: "Victim-blaming runs rampant in headlines and news features, sexual assault is often misnamed or mischaracterized, and women's behavior is treated with more scrutiny than rapists' crimes."[80] Her "rules for journalists" include not describing rape as "sex"; not perpetuating race, class, gender, or sexual stereotypes, especially with reference to nonwhite, queer, trans, immigrant, or other marginalized communities; consulting experts who can provide informed context about sexual assault; and emphasizing the fact that rape is caused by the perpetrators, not by the victims.

Valenti, of course, is not the first to call out this issue or to offer correctives: feminist scholars and activists have been acutely aware of journalism's role in perpetuating rape culture. Over the past three decades they have not only identified patterns of rape culture in reporting, but developed clear guidelines for better practices. Yet, for decades, this informed and in-depth analysis and the attendant antidotes have gone largely unheeded by the press.

Journalists and the topic of rape go back a long way, and the relationship has generally been a toxic one. In the southern United States before the Civil War, for example, newspapers were "rabidly vicious"[81] in their reporting of alleged rapes of white women by black men. By covering lynchings in graphic detail and by insisting on the guilt of the black men accused, news reporting was specifically intended to "arouse prurient interest, engage racist citizens, and uphold a social order that was dependent on the systematic oppression of Blacks by Whites."[82]

Indeed, throughout the nineteenth century "journalism

feasted on a steady diet of vice coverage and sexual scandal," as newspapers discovered that "sex and death dramatically increased circulation rates."[83] In turn-of-the-twentieth-century America, newspapers stirred up a panic over "white slavery": this was an apocryphal story about the kidnapping of white women as part of a sexual slave trade, and it served to reinforce racism and tighten social restrictions on white women's sexual autonomy.[84]

In England, too, Victorian-era newspapers ramped up their reporting on "sports, gossip, crime and sex" mainly in order to attract mass audiences.[85] In one famous early example of reporting on sex crimes, William T. Stead, editor of the *Pall Mall Gazette* in England, ran a series on child prostitution in 1885.[86] The sensational and partly fabricated series flew off newsstands, and also resulted in the passage of "Stead's Act," which legislated against child prostitution and raised the age of consent from 13 to 16. While this might be thought of as a progressive outcome, the historian Deborah Gorham argues that it served principally to control "the unruly behavior of girls"[87] whom it was seeking to protect, while ignoring the economic and social conditions that may have pushed them into prostitution at such young ages.

Not long afterwards, London newspapers' coverage of Jack the Ripper in 1888 seized on the opportunity to ramp up sensational storytelling. The Ripper's infamously gruesome crimes involved raping and murdering prostitutes after slashing out their sexual organs. News accounts seized on the gore as well as on the opportunity to demean London's then working-class

Whitechapel district as a criminal domain filled with sinister foreign others. Newspaper editors defended their salacious coverage with the claim that disclosing graphic details of the murders might elicit information leading to an arrest, although no such result transpired. The Ripper's identity remains unknown to this day.

Even in contemporary times, journalists declare idealistic motives for their work. "Journalists see their profession as an altruistic one in which they serve the public by providing information that helps them make sense of the world," note the media scholars Homero Gil de Zúñiga and Amber Hinsley.[88] Investigative journalism, in particular, seeks to expose wrongdoing so as to redress it through social change.

Challenging and changing social wrongs necessarily involves reporting on crime, and sex crimes are so endemic in most societies that journalists are virtually obligated to cover them. But news coverage of rape has been fraught with problems since its inception, shoring up rape myths and reinforcing rape culture under the cloak of authority and verisimilitude. Feminist analyses of news about sexual violence have identified problematic patterns, for example focusing on sensational or extraordinary cases while neglecting everyday domestic violence; victim-blaming and holding victims responsible for the rapists' violence; overemphasizing the character and credibility of the victim; normalizing violence against women and other vulnerable people; and sympathizing with the male perpetrators.[89]

Feminist activists and scholars have also developed guidelines for good practice in reporting on sexual violence. Decades ago, the media scholar Marian

Meyers wrote: "If the news is to stop contributing to the epidemic of violence against women and actually work to eradicate it, journalists must take responsibility for halting the perpetuation of myths and stereotypes that underlie patriarchal ideology and the mythology of anti-women violence."[90] Her suggestions for taking steps in that direction include not identifying rape victims by name; not including details of the victim's appearance, character, or sexual history; taking all forms of sexual violence seriously; and being sensitive to intersectional issues of race and class. The reporter Debra McKinney, who has covered sexual violence herself, advises defining rape in terms of violence and trauma, avoiding lurid details in covering the story, and providing resources to help survivors.[91] Maggie Wykes advises against blaming victims and other women, such as mothers of victims, while minimizing the role of male perpetrators.[92] The journalist Helen Benedict admonishes reporters for reinforcing rape myths that blame and stigmatize survivors; she advocates increased care about the language that is used, so that it might not wrongly suggest that the victim deserved or enjoyed the assault; contextualizing the assault; and following up with the survivor.[93] This steady drumbeat of feminist analysis and critique has just very recently begun to spark change: journalists and editors are becoming more aware of, and attentive to, the need for a thoughtful and informed approach to covering sexual assault.

And in recent years investigative journalism has proven that it can be a force for uncovering rape culture and its pernicious impact. This became painfully clear at the 2018 trial of the serial sexual abuser Larry Nassar, where courtroom audiences sobbed openly during days of victim testimony. Nassar was the Olympic doctor convicted of abusing more than 500 girls who were athletes in his care, and his trial was a compelling MeToo moment. It occurred just a few months after the #MeToo social media storm had erupted nationally and then worldwide, and it revealed not only the depravity of one "sick" male but the collusion of powerful institutions that deliberately abetted his crimes, contributing to a culture where rape was condoned.

Nassar's conviction was a watershed event, especially at the moment of Justice Rosemarie Aquilina's piercing declaration, "I just signed your death warrant," when she sentenced him to up to 175 years in prison.[94] In addition to victim testimonies and accounts of institutional malfeasance that were included in both the print and the broadcast coverage of the trial, the revelations of wrongdoing were actually set in motion by journalists. In fact it was reporting by the *Indianapolis Star* newspaper that spurred the gymnast Rachael Denhollander to file the first criminal complaint against Nassar's sexual abuse. She was also the first to publicly disclose, in the *IndyStar*, her victimization at the hands of Nassar, opening the way for the hundreds of testaments and lawsuits that followed.

Representation in the news media was thus a powerful force for creating survivors' solidarity, as it mobilized an awareness of their shared experience, identified this shared experience as criminal sexual abuse (which many of them had not previously understood), and signaled the need for public disclosure as well as for legal action. In fact the Nassar testimonies had a domino effect, inspiring the disclosure of sexual abuse of male wrestlers at Ohio State University. "Michigan State is what got us to say, 'Hey, it can happen even to guys,'" wrestler Nick Nutter told the *New York Times*.[95]

The *Boston Globe*'s prize-winning investigation into child sexual abuse in the Catholic Church had had similar outcomes. Starting in 2002, the *Globe*'s "Spotlight" team used church documents to reveal the widespread and deliberately concealed rape of children by priests. As with the *IndyStar*, the *Globe*'s first stories included a hotline that people could call to report sexual abuse by the clergy. "What happened was, over the next couple of weeks, just in Boston, 300 victims of priests called to tell us their stories," recalled lead reporter Walter Robinson. "Many of these victims had never told anyone because they felt all this shame and guilt as children when it happened to them."[96] The number of victims coming forward snowballed; the *Globe* published over 900 stories on the systemically protected pedophilia within the Catholic Church, a global hotbed of rape culture. Lawsuits against the church followed. In the United States alone, at this writing, major settlements and monetary awards for priests' sexual abuse total over $3 billion. The Catholic Church is also beginning to make structural changes that will counter child sexual abuse by priests, including the creation of the Pontifical Commission for the Protection of Minors. The damage to the victims is irreparable. But it might never have been revealed or redressed without investigative journalism.

The same year Nassar was convicted, the *Miami Herald* published a three-part investigative story about a sex-trafficking ring run by the financier Jeffrey Epstein, who raped hundreds of underage girls, some as young as 13. Despite compelling evidence of Epstein's serial predations, the US Attorney for Southern Florida at the time, Alexander Acosta, struck a plea deal that allowed Epstein to escape with a ludicrously light sentence. The plea halted an ongoing FBI probe into Epstein's sex crimes; and his victims were never told of the deal. It was only the *Herald* reporter Julie K. Brown and her deeply researched reporting on the case that reopened the investigation a decade later, with the result that charges of federal sex trafficking were filed against Epstein in 2019. Brown's series *Perversion of Justice* impelled the reopening of the case and Epstein's eventual indictment. Like the "Spotlight" investigation and the *IndyStar*'s reportage, it revealed how rape culture permeates organizational systems and operates to protect even the most flagrant and ruthless sexual offenders.

Just before Brown's series broke, Jodi Kantor and Megan Twohey of the *New York Times* and Ronan Farrow of the *New Yorker* revealed Harvey Weinstein's long history of sexually assaulting women who worked with him, some of them high-profile actors. These accounts also detailed the institutional collusion of major film corporations, of the criminal justice system, and of legal strategists, all of which conspired to cover up Weinstein's crimes and to silence the survivors.

In working on these stories, the journalists were acutely aware of their responsibilities to survivors and of the critical need for careful and informed reporting and writing. As she began searching for survivors of

Epstein's predations, Julie K. Brown said that she was concerned that she "was going to retraumatize them by contacting them out of the blue."[97] That a journalist would even be alert to the possibility of retraumatization marks a progressive shift in reportorial sensitivity to rape survivors. The *Boston Globe* "Spotlight" reporters were similarly aware of survivors: "What was not in the [Church] documents was any indication anywhere of concern for the children who had been harmed. Not *anywhere*," noted the *Globe*'s Walter Robinson, who mentioned this indifference in his story.[98] The abuse "wrecked survivors in a way they could never recover from, or that they still struggle to recover from, at age forty, fifty, sixty," said reporter Sasha Pfeiffer.[99] The inclusion of hotlines and survivors' resources in the stories was intended to help victims access the support and therapy they needed. In another signal moment, the reporting followed feminist scholars' guidelines—a lasting breakthrough for scholarship's contributions to social change. Most news stories of gender or sexual violence now routinely include information on resources for survivors.

The stories were also conscious of class as a factor in the sexual violence. In her reporting for the *Miami Herald*, Brown noted that Epstein's victims were from underprivileged backgrounds and precarious family situations: "at a time when Olympic gymnasts and Hollywood actors have become a catalyst for a cultural reckoning about sexual abuse, Epstein's victims have all but been forgotten,"[100] she wrote, going on to quote one of the victims as saying that Epstein "preyed on girls who were in a bad way, girls who were basically homeless."[101] The *Globe* reporters were also sensitive to the fact that children from poor families were targeted for priests' abuse. In an important shift, the stories never blamed the survivors or their families for their victimization: instead, responsibility was squarely laid upon the perpetrators and the institutional systems that had enabled the criminal behavior.

Kate Wells, whose Michigan Public Radio series *Believed* won a Peabody Award for its chronicling of the Larry Nassar case, said that the survivors educated her about sexual assault.[102] Listening to and acknowledging the credibility of survivors' accounts shaped the reporting in ways that repudiated the rape culture framework. At the same time, reporters were meticulous about verifying their sources' accounts, combing through court documents and other evidence, and corroborating the facts. This reportorial care may have been a response to the fiasco that ensued after *Rolling Stone* magazine had published "A Rape on Campus" just a few years earlier. *Rolling Stone*'s graphic account of a gang rape on the University of Virginia campus was proven to be substantively false and embroiled the magazine in multimillion dollar defamation suits once the story had to be retracted. *Rolling Stone*'s eagerness to trust the survivor and to indict the university represented an overbalancing toward anti-rape activism[103] that could in principle damage the credibility of other survivors willing to speak about their assaults. The *Rolling Stone* fiasco underscores the need for rigorous journalistic practice, fact checking, and editorial oversight—in addition to familiarity with best practices for reporting on sexual violence. As Jodi Kantor of the

New York Times said, "everything needs to be scrutinized; everything needs to be checked ... the best way to get people to believe women is to document those women's stories really thoroughly."[104]

Truth can have unforeseen consequences. One outcome of the *IndyStar*'s reporting was some survivors' realization, after reading the stories, that they had been sexually assaulted. Because Larry Nassar had convinced the girls that his forcible penetration of their bodies was medically necessary, many of them had not identified their experiences as sexual abuse and therefore had not sought counseling despite suffering post-rape trauma. But the *IndyStar* chose language for the stories with the goal of clarifying the definition of sexual abuse, describing in anatomical detail what Nassar had done. The newspaper's Marisa Kwiatkowski said they grappled with the decision:

> [T]here was more than one debate in the newsroom about how to describe the crimes accurately. For the public to understand what Nassar did to these young women, I believe we should describe what he did briefly but explicitly ... Since "sexual abuse" can mean many things, I believe it should be clear that Nassar inserted his fingers inside women's vaginas, and sometimes their anuses, without gloves, lubricant or consent, often while their parents were in the room. All the women testified in court what he did to them so I believe we have a responsibility to report the words they used and be part of the culture that sheds light on sexual violence so it doesn't stay in the shadows.[105]

The *IndyStar*'s clarity and candor, while controversial,

ended up enlightening survivors and emboldening them to come forward even as it educated readers about the parameters of criminal sexual abuse. For the same reason, the *Globe* similarly decided to be specific in its reported details of priests' assaults on children. The reporters were neither casual nor gratuitous in their use of language. The specificity was the result of carefully considered choices intended to support the survivors and to aid in the criminal prosecutions of perpetrators.

The journalistic breakthroughs that have begun to reveal and denounce rape culture in our societies should be thought of as a first step. They offer a glimmer of hope of channeling the considerable power of the press as a force for combatting sexual violence. But they have barely scratched the surface of rape culture as it operates in the United States, not to mention other regions and contexts across the globe. The columnist Katha Pollitt urges us to think about the invisibility of women and, by extension, of others "who have not entered the folklore of crime because their beatings and/or rapes and/or murders lacked the appropriate ingredients for full-dress media treatment—which include, alas, being white, young, middle-class, and, as the tabloids love to say, 'attractive.'"[106]

For journalists, this differential should be a crucial issue, if the true goal of investigative work is to expose wrongdoing and remedy social ills. Available data indicate that women of color and LGBTQ people experience extremely high rates of sexual violence (and the true incidence is likely much higher, given that most sexual violence is not reported.)[107] A recent study shows that men are more likely to sexually target black women at work, because the latter "are perceived as having relatively little power in workplaces, and are therefore viewed as being less likely to file a complaint."[108] For women of color, a variety of intersecting factors—social, cultural, historical—constrain their ability to report sexual victimization. In addition to concerns that are shared by many sexual violence survivors, such as fears of not being believed or treated fairly by authorities, women of color face specific barriers to reporting. African American women might hesitate to report because of the "strong black woman" myth that ties them to stoicism and silence, or because of a "cultural mandate to protect African American male offenders,"[109] who are disproportionately penalized in American criminal justice. Women from Asian cultural backgrounds do not report sexual violence for fear of losing their reputation or their family's reputation, or of being ostracized by their communities.[110] Almost 80 percent of American Indian and Native Alaskan women experience sexual violence, but reporting is difficult in small tribal communities, and a maze of federal, tribal, and state laws creates almost insurmountable legal barriers for them. "As a consequence, Indigenous women are denied justice. And the perpetrators are going unpunished," notes an Amnesty International report.[111] Latina women may face language barriers, fear of deportation if their immigration status is unstable, or victim blaming within their families.[112] Trans people experience "shocking[ly] high levels of sexual abuse and assault,"[113] but few report it; one study indicated that the low rates of reporting in trans communities were due to the fact that perpetrators are often law enforcement officers, social workers, or health care providers.[114] In fact, a growing consciousness among anti-rape activists recognizes state-sanctioned authorities and policies as contributing to sexual and other violence against communities of color, which raises questions about the effectiveness of these authorities and policies in solving the problem.

Given all this, it is clear that journalism's MeToo moment cannot end with the victories of wealthy white women; it must not end in continued reportorial myopia about the sexual violence experienced every day by women of color, poor women, immigrant women, women with disabilities, LGBTQ people, children of all genders and sexual orientations, and men. For journalists of integrity and vision, a vast array of untold stories and unknown victims awaits compassionate attention. As Alice Walker queries in her short story "Advancing Luna—and Ida B. Wells," "Who knows what the black woman thinks of rape? Who has asked her? Who *cares*?"[115]

3
Resistance

Reckonings

In 1851, a *New York Daily Times* editorial lambasted the women's suffrage movement for being excessively demanding: "We regret to see how obstinately our American women are bent on appropriating more than their fair share of Constitutional privileges. ... We are clearly of the opinion that the time has come for the organization of a 'Rights of Man' Association to withstand the greedy oppressiveness of womankind. ... Anti-masculine agitation must be stayed by some means."[1]

Almost two centuries later, in much the same vein, the MeToo movement faces charges of going "too far"[2] in its "unquestioning condemnation of men accused of sexual insensitivity"[3] and in its "lynch-mob mentality and repudiation of due process."[4] In various quarters, as the MeToo movement has gathered momentum, it has been met with an equal and opposite reaction.

The backlash against the MeToo movement rests on a variety of claims, the most common of which asserts that women's outrage over sexual misconduct is irrationally broad, blind to the differences between sexual violence and lesser lapses such as catcalls or flirting. Other repudiators of MeToo decry the "victim" narrative that positions women as lacking any sexual agency or responsibility. The movement is also framed, like the suffrage movement, as being radically anti-male in its supposed characterization of all masculinity as inherently "toxic."

These charges are worth taking seriously. They expose real anxieties about a powerful feminist social movement that, like the suffrage movement, upends the gender norms and sexual hierarchies we've taken for granted, revealing painful truths about sex, power, and violence. The criticisms invite close scrutiny of the movement's ethics, goals, and vision. They compel us to examine the scope of rape culture. They raise the specter of a bogeyman—a raving "victim/vigilante feminist," who insists that all accusations are de facto true and seeks to destroy all men as inherent sexual predators; but that figure can be confronted and defused without jettisoning the movement and its potential for progressive social change.

Most of the condemnations of MeToo are based on personal anecdotes: a man who was fired for denying a woman a raise after she ended their relationship; an HR complaint that was made about a well-intentioned compliment or an accidental touch. These are cautionary tales, used to demonstrate how the new consciousness of sexual misconduct results in rushing to unfair judgment and penalizing men for naïve or innocuous behaviors.

The case of the comedian Aziz Ansari, too, provoked widespread criticism of MeToo as overwrought hysteria. This case came to light in 2018, when the now defunct website babe.net published a lengthy story detailing a 22-year-old woman's first date with the comedian. The story, recounted to a reporter, described how Ansari reportedly pressured Grace (a pseudonym) into unwanted sexual activities.[5] The story rapidly went viral and the case was hotly debated as a "MeToo moment." Opinions were split: the incident was seen by some as exposing the embeddedness of male sexual opportunism and disregard for mutual assent, by others as a paradigm of women's incapacity to distinguish between a "bad date" and sexual assault. Writing in the *Atlantic*, the journalist Caitlin Flanagan noted that the story served as "an important contribution to the present conversation" through the intense reactions it generated, but in her view Ansari was "assassinated, on the basis of one woman's anonymous account," and his career destroyed by some kind of "revenge porn." Moreover, she read the tale as racist, as an attack by a privileged white woman on a Muslim man of color.[6] On the other hand, many women saw the incident as revealing a culture in which male coercion is normalized and women's attempts to stave off unwelcome advances are disregarded—in fact, a rape culture. The matter was complicated by Ansari's *soi-disant* feminism and vaunted support for MeToo and Time's Up.

As Flanagan notes, the incident is worth interrogating as an exemplar, because its polarizing effect surfaces the core complexities of heterosex today. Flanagan's critique invoked a traditional gendered script in which men are sexual aggressors and women are resisters, obligated to forcefully reject unwanted male propositions; she derided Grace's feeblemindedness in not energetically "getting away from a man who was trying to pressure her into sex" she didn't want.[7] Her critique echoed that of others, who found Grace's claim of assault murky at best. From this perspective, if the action fails to follow a clear-cut script—wherein women's agency is construed in terms of an immediate either/or acceptance or rejection of sexual advance from a man—then the woman is to blame for not having expressed her will clearly.

But individual sexual encounters don't occur in a social vacuum, and prevailing models of heterosexuality shape and constrain the way things play out in real-world situations. "In a culture saturated with the rhetoric of choice, it can be an uncomfortable realization that some choices are perhaps not *really* choices at all," writes the psychologist Nicola Gavey.[8] In her analysis, the normative expectations of sex in relationships, along with the traditional "male sexual drive discourse," can produce situations in which women do not believe they have the right to refuse sex. And indeed, in the Aziz Ansari story, the pseudonymous survivor Grace said: "It took a really long time for me to validate this as sexual assault. And that's why I confronted so many of my friends and listened to what they had to say, because I wanted validation that it was actually bad."[9]

Gavey recognizes this uncertainty:

> Many women have talked to me about experiences that they didn't call rape, but which I find difficult to see as just sex. They include stories of situations in which a man applied pressure that fell short of actual or threatened physical force, but which the woman felt unable to resist, as well as encounters where a man was rough and brutish, and the woman described letting sex happen because she felt unable to stop it. They also include stories of situations where a male partner was not directly coercive at all, but where the woman nevertheless found herself going along with sex that was neither desired nor enjoyed because she did not feel it was her right to stop it or because she did not know how to refuse. All of these accounts in different ways point to a complex gray area between what we might think of as mutually consenting sex, on the one hand, and rape or sexual coercion on the other.[10]

There are important distinctions to recognize along a continuum from coercion to violent assault. It is, however, important to point out that gray areas must be acknowledged and interrogated, as they are part of a changing sexual landscape in which women, in particular, seek new models for mutually pleasurable and unequivocally assenting sex.

In this sense, Grace's story of her date with Aziz Ansari can be interpreted as something other than "revenge porn." It is instead a daring venture into new territory, a revelation of vulnerability and confusion in a situation that was obviously construed differently along gendered lines. For Grace, the sex was coerced. According to the babe.net story, she tried to send Ansari nonverbal cues signaling her reluctance to engage in sex by moving away and going still; she even said, "I don't want to feel forced because then I'll hate you, and I don't want to hate you."[11] Ansari persisted in demanding sexual activity, perhaps assuming from her presence in his apartment, or because he had bought her dinner, that she was available for sex. These interpretations are, very likely, the outcome of historically entrenched gender roles and expectations that take new forms in an era of apparent sexual liberation and casual hookups. Both gender and sex, the philosopher Judith Butler has argued, are performative, produced through "acts, gestures, enactments"[12] that are not always consciously transacted but rather derived from "a sedimentation of gender norms"[13] in a society's history. We are subconsciously guided by these norms; public beliefs and discourses about gender and sex shape our behaviors, becoming internalized in ways that can tilt the balance in tricky situations. And when clear thought is occluded by anxiety or fear, the tilt is often toward conformity rather than resistance.

Rape myths are also at work in this scenario: the myth that women mean "yes" when they say "no" to sex is still prevalent. "Indeed, men's belief in token resistance can be used as justification for not stopping sexual activity despite a woman's protests," according to one study of rape myths and their impact.[14] And, even today, many men believe that, if they pay for dinner, a sexual quid pro quo is reasonable.[15] It is entirely probable that these belief systems were operating in the Ansari scenario. Rape myths, which take the form of norms and discourses, have bolstered patriarchal hierarchies over time, undermining women's power to define the parameters of sex. Thus, from Grace's perspective, the situation was coercive and the sex unwanted; from Ansari's, it was not. But if even one participant felt pressured and unwilling, it was not consensual.

Some of the controversy centered on the fact that Grace did not reject Ansari's advances forcefully or physically: she did not shout, push him, hit him, or run. Her lack of force seems to cast doubt on whether the encounter was a "real" sexual assault. This kind of questioning of the victim's response directly affects women's credibility when they report sexual assaults. But research shows that, "faced with sexual coercion, women adopt nonforceful behaviors in their attempt to stop the behavior."[16] Moreover, in a social environment where men's violence against women is an ever present possibility, women are not sure what a refusal will engender and, as a result, may capitulate to unwanted sex. Nonetheless, Grace tried several times to let Ansari know that she was not interested in sex, and he apparently plowed right past her cues.

All this raises the specter of "consent," a highly charged and complicated concept in the area of rape and in rape culture. It is "consent" that is invoked in refuting claims of sexual assault in legal proceedings and "consent" that is deemed to be the most powerful marker of the character of a sexual encounter. Yet, as the philosopher Susan Brison points out,

> There is no parallel to this in the case of other crimes, such as theft or murder. … In the cases of both theft and murder, the notion of violation is built into our conceptions of the physical acts constituting the crimes, so it

> is inconceivable that one could consent to the act in question. Why is it so easy ... to think of rape, however, as "normal sexual activity minus consent?"[17]

Women's refusal is constantly and tortuously questioned, and their consent is indiscriminately inferred from their clothing, whereabouts, level of inebriation, word choice, body language, and countless other hypothetical signs, rather than from their actual first-hand accounts of what happened, or even from existing evidence. In no other crime is consent even a plausible idea. Only rape victims bear the burden of proving that they did not consent to being attacked.

The philosopher Ann Cahill reminds us that "most women can generally and with relative ease distinguish between acts of rape and consensual, mutually desired heterosexual sex."[18] The legal scholar Catharine MacKinnon has recently argued for a recognition of "welcomed sex," as opposed to using "consent" as a stand-in for desire. "In social reality, the crucible of meaning, sex that is actually desired or wanted or welcomed is never termed consensual. ... No one says, 'We had a great hot night. She (or I or we) consented.'"[19] There is growing agreement, among feminist scholars of sexual violence, that "consent" is an untenable standard for assessing the veracity of sexual assault, as it fails to take into account the power dynamics that frame sex and constrain agency, especially for women during heterosexual activity. The Aziz Ansari incident brings the problems around "consent" into sharp focus.

One of the charges against the Aziz Ansari story is that its publication wrecked the comedian's career. This is a criticism also aimed at the MeToo movement: that it goads women to make hasty and unverified accusations of sexual misconduct, thwarting due process and excessively penalizing men for possibly invented infractions. This criticism needs to be taken seriously because, if true, the movement could indeed have unjust and dire consequences for men. Yet, to date, few charges of sexual assault have been proven to be baseless or false, and in fact most sexual assaults are never reported at all.[20] On the other hand, despite its "Believe Women" slogan, the MeToo movement has never insisted that all reports of sexual assault are unquestionably true. The *Washington Post* points out: "From the beginning, many #MeToo activists emphasized that while accusers should be taken seriously and treated respectfully, that did not mean they should be believed without question."[21] Indeed, the journalists who broke the Harvey Weinstein story that dovetailed with the MeToo movement's 2017 revival have emphasized the importance of fact checking and verification. More importantly, MeToo's real goal is to support survivors rather than to bring men down—as Tarana Burke has repeatedly emphasized.[22]

The goal of ending sexual violence involves reenvisioning sexuality so that it involves an ethical and equitable interaction. The psychologist Nicola Gavey calls for us to "imagine a world in which heterosex could be configured differently."[23] Interestingly, the Aziz Ansari incident seems to have begun to do just that. Rather than being ruined, Ansari has had continued success. He has publicly expressed regret that he caused Grace pain, and he admits that the incident and its aftermath caused him to rethink his behavior toward women. He builds these reflections into his live shows and televised standup routines. His self-examination and remorse are indicators that the movement is not "against men"; it is intended to include men in the process of changing rape culture. The activist and scholar Jackson Katz tells us that male allyship (on which see https://theantioppressionnetwork.com/allyship) is crucial in preventing and ending sexual violence: "When we ask men to reject sexism and the abuse of women, we are not taking something away from them. In fact, we are giving them something very valuable—a vision of manhood that does not depend on putting down others in order to lift itself up."[24]

Granular scrutiny of the Aziz Ansari story and of its significance has elicited a great deal of public discourse about desire, consent, and rape culture. This kind of consciousness raising is a first step toward changing the game. The ongoing MeToo revelations of sexual misconduct, abuse, and assault—and the thoughtful conversations they prompt—are necessary way stations on a trajectory toward a new sexual ethics of equity and nonviolence.

Redress

A more trenchant rebuke of #MeToo centers on its alignment with existing legal and criminal justice systems, which have long been recognized as fraught with racism, homophobia, transphobia, and misogyny. "While #MeToo has ruptured a pervasive silence around sexual assault," writes the scholar V. Jo Hsu, "it has also done so largely through a vocabulary of criminalization and carceral punishment."[25] Seen in this light, the MeToo movement calls for an intersectional analysis of its political and ethical commitments.

The legal and juridical outcomes of MeToo are defining features of the movement. For many, the infamous "perp walk" of serial rapist and movie mogul Harvey Weinstein was a triumph, caught on camera by many news outlets and circulated worldwide. Weinstein is a symbol of the movement's impact, his indictment for rape in the third degree plus a criminal sexual act rendering him "the first of the high-profile men accused of sexual misconduct since October 2017 to face genuine legal consequences for his actions"—to be investigated, charged, and tried, all within the world created by the MeToo movement.[26] Other convictions of sex offenders such as Bill Cosby and Larry Nassar followed the Weinstein trial. Roger Ailes, the Fox News chairman, paid massive legal settlements to women who had brought suit against him for sexual harassment. The toll from these legal cases has amounted to billions of dollars in awards and settlements, paid out by corporations, universities, and the perpetrators themselves.

At one level, the financial remunerations paid to survivors and the jail sentences meted out to these men are a vindication for the women they had assaulted, as well as for others. (The philosopher Susan Brison comments: "Sexual violence victimizes not only those women who are directly attacked but *all* women."[27]) Yet even as women have expressed satisfaction at seeing their assailants put behind bars, they have also embraced the social and structural changes the verdicts heralded. Janice Baker-Kinney, a Cosby survivor, said: "This may be the end for Mr. Cosby, but it is the beginning for many of us, to fight for justice, to do the right thing and support every person who has ever been blamed and shamed and humiliated."[28] The actor Rose McGowan declared she saw the Weinstein verdict as "a huge step forward in our collective healing,"[29] presaging a "cultural reset."[30]

In this way, the legal penalties imposed on the offenders were construed as contributing to widespread support for survivors and a validation of their credibility. The verdicts in fact did mark a change in a legal system that has traditionally minimized the seriousness of rape as a crime—in general, "convictions for rape are the exception to the rule."[31] Powerful and wealthy men tend to be shielded by legal institutions and processes, and allegations against them are frequently discredited or downplayed. So the sentencing of Weinstein, Cosby, Epstein, Nassar, and others did signal a certain shift in the zeitgeist, affirming survivors' truths and the reality of their ordeals.

Yet, as has been widely noted, the survivors in these cases were mainly wealthy heterosexual white women, which does not diminish the gravity of their assaults but likely does factor into the success of their legal actions. These women fit the mold of the "believable victim" in terms of race, class, sexual orientation, and appearance. As movie stars, TV personalities, and Olympic athletes, they were revered as icons. And, even so, it took years for them to gather the courage to report their experiences, and even longer for the legal process to play out. When it did, Weinstein was not convicted on all counts, Cosby was freed by a hung jury before being convicted in a retrial, and Epstein died under mysterious circumstances before he could be sentenced. Only Larry Nassar, the doctor who assaulted more than 150 women, faced immediate and severe sentencing, from a woman judge, for criminal sexual conduct.

Still, the news of their prison terms was met with gratitude and a sense of vindication; headlines were celebratory; optimism ran high and future victories were predicted for sexual assault survivors. The symbolism of legal penalties for these serial sexual abusers was significant in a culture where incarceration stands for justice, particularly in the case of violent crimes.

But a countercurrent of thought, going back decades, views prison as actually *opposing* justice in a range of ways. To begin with, the racism of the US penal system is an established matter. "Racial disparity defines contemporary American mass incarceration," writes the political scientist Alex Zamalin.[32] "For anyone who studies criminal justice in the United States, the problem of the disproportionate arrest and incarceration of African Americans and, to a lesser extent, Latinos, looms large," observes the sociologist Heather Schoenfeld.[33] "In states where Native Americans comprise a relatively large part of the population, they are disproportionately represented in the prison system," according to a report from Cornell University's Roosevelt Institute, which also notes that Native men are four times more likely to go to jail than white men, and Native women six times more likely than white women.[34]

Within this overall context of racism's influence on arrests and sentencing, sexual violence brings additional intersectional factors into play. Race, class, gender and gender identity, and sexual orientation work in complexly enmeshed ways to affect juridical processes related to sexual abuse, assault, and harassment. These issues are further complicated by disability, citizenship status, and other social vectors. Sexual violence is vastly underreported on the whole, and all these additional factors affect survivors' probability of reporting, with the result that rapes of white women by black men are the most likely assaults to even *be* reported, as they are perceived by authorities to be the most credible.[35] And the legal system "is expected to afford the greatest leniency to White men who sexually assault Black women."[36]

Even when reports are made, the police have the discretion to decide whether a crime has occurred. They can decide whether to make an arrest. Studies indicate that it is less likely that a reported sexual assault against a person of color would make it to prosecution.[37]

Sexual orientation and gender identity also intersect with race in ways that further impede the chances of sexual assaults being recognized as "valid." Same-sex sexual violence is denied or minimized by authorities, read as volitional because it may occur in the context of a same-sex relationship, and challenged because the incidents vary so much from the myth of "real rape."[38] Trans people endure even greater discrimination in the criminal justice system on multiple fronts: sexual violence against them tends to be dismissed, as they are not considered to be "believable victims,"[39] so they cannot easily find police assistance or legal help when they experience rape or sex abuse. Yet, at the same time, trans people are disproportionately subject to policing and imprisonment for a variety of reasons.[40] They are frequently victims of sexual violence at the hands of police, prison guards, and other inmates. Research shows that "transgender inmates have dramatically higher rates of sexual assault and rape than the average prisoner," writes the attorney Kylar Broadus.[41]

The sentencing of Weinstein, Cosby, and Nassar, then, cannot be viewed in simple terms. It would be short-sighted and unthinking to celebrate their convictions only as victories that predict justice for all sexual assault victims and survivors. Given the weight of the historical, social, and cultural factors that shape legal interpretations of sexual violence, there is slim likelihood of marginalized people's assaults finding the same level of judicial support. The deck is stacked against survivors who are poor, come from communities of color, are LGBTQ, and are undocumented or disabled—in any permutation or combination of these characteristics. For them, even the possibility of reporting sexual violence is diminished; and follow-ups are uncertain. The survivors themselves may experience harsh treatment in a system that routinely fails to validate the reality or gravity of their sexual victimization.

Yet the outcomes of the high-profile cases of Weinstein and others have been pivotal in terms of enacting structural change. They have altered the legal terrain so as to actually validate the testimony of women and penalize the sexual criminality of wealthy and powerful men. These cases did mark a shift; and they do make a difference. The legal wins have percolated to less rarefied environments than the media industries: for example, an Iowa court awarded a settlement of $2.2 million to a woman who blew the whistle on rampant sexual harassment in the state legislature.[42] But the question remains: How meaningful are the impacts of these cases, given the problematic context of the legal and judicial systems?

These complexities bring up important matters for the MeToo movement and, indeed, for everyone seeking to end sexual violence. Since 2017, #MeToo has blurred into MeToo, such that the two—hashtag and movement—have become practically indistinguishable. This blurring has commingled their commitments, ethics, and goals. But these conceptual groundings need to be carefully parsed, as the path to ending sexual violence depends on them.

#MeToo is linked to the Time's Up organization, which was founded by women in the Hollywood entertainment industry. The organization conducts research and develops policy on gender-related issues such as pay equity and childcare, and also funds legal actions "to help survivors of sexual harassment and retaliation, especially low-income women and people of color, achieve justice."[43] Time's Up has followed through with a variety of initiatives: a class action sexual harassment lawsuit against the McDonald's fast-food chain, advocacy for stronger anti-sexual harassment laws, and a study of voting trends (among other actions). While Time's Up endorses a range of reforms and cultural changes aimed at ending sexual discrimination and violence, its legal advocacy ties it to "carceral feminism,"[44] which achieves gender justice through criminal justice. The feminist media scholar Michelle Rodino-Colocino sees

Time's Up as motivated by empathy for underrepresented and marginalized people; she writes that, even as empathy can motivate structural change, "structural change may also advance empathy for girls and women of color who are victim-survivors."[45]

On the other hand, feminist voices are increasingly challenging legal recourse as an effective deterrent to sex crimes; and they make a particularly sharp critique of incarceration. For decades, the feminist scholar Angela Davis has argued for the elimination of prisons, describing them as places where "ever larger numbers of people from racially oppressed communities" are relegated to "an isolated existence marked by authoritarian regimes, violence, disease, and technologies of seclusion that produce severe mental instability."[46] Following Foucault, the gender scholar Chloë Taylor argues that prisons *constitute* criminals rather than reforming them: "the real function of the prison has been to transform politicized offenders into psychiatrized and stigmatized delinquents."[47] The brutality of prison, particularly toward society's most vulnerable people, causes great harm; and that harm is compounded when prisoners are released without employment prospects, education, financial resources, or emotional support. Moreover, prisons themselves are sites of horrific levels of sexual violence. "Prison ... normalizes rape in a population that will, for the most part, return to the outside world," writes Taylor.[48] Ultimately, structural changes that overlook the violence, biases, and inequities of the criminal justice system itself will do little to advance the cause of survivors, who are routinely failed by it.

Emerging models of anti-violence activism "empower marginalized survivors" and outline "more imaginative, ground-up enactments of justice."[49] These models extend the concept of validating survivors' voices by starting with survivors' needs and preferences about justice—which often don't involve police or prison. The grassroots organization INCITE!, which works on behalf of women of color to end violence, supports a model of community accountability in which communities collectively develop "sustainable strategies to address community members' abusive behavior, creating a process for them to account for their actions and transform their behavior."[50] Along similar lines, the masculinity scholar and activist Jackson Katz has long advocated for bystander intervention training for men as an effective way to challenge rape culture and to prevent rape.[51] This recognition needs to be integrated with feminist, queer, and trans approaches, so that women and LGBTQ people are not sidelined in anti-violence activism but collaborate with male allies in bystander and other interventions against sexual violence.[52] Some scholars invoke the powerful concept of "trans" frameworks—which encompass transgender, transnational, and transformative consciousness—to develop progressive ways of ending sexual abuse, assault, and harassment. A "trans" perspective recognizes the workings of structural power in violence as it is manifested in gendered and sexual relations, border politics, racism, disability and other modes of embodiment, and resource allocation.[53]

If the goals of #MeToo and Time's Up are mobilized by empathy for, and solidarity with, survivors, then the reforms they seek should address the criminal justice system itself, not just corporations and media representations. "How can it be a feminist remedy to consign rapists to institutions where they are at grave risk of rape themselves?" queries the legal scholar Constance Backhouse. "If we are against rape, we are against all rape."[54] As anti-rape movements with significant resources, reach, and visibility, #MeToo and Time's Up have the potential to disrupt and transform concepts of justice for sexual violence survivors.

Tarana Burke has emphasized that the ethical basis of the MeToo movement is "a collective vision to see a world free of sexual violence," so that "every human being has the right to walk through this life with their humanity fully intact."[55] MeToo is grounded in validating and addressing the real experiences of those most vulnerable to the misuse of power and privilege. Its focus has never been on pursuing criminal penalties for perpetrators—a recognition that reveals a contradiction between MeToo and #MeToo.

To reflect on this raises a number of questions. Are there less punitive and more thoughtful reparations that could recompense survivors for their suffering? Does the sentencing of a few white men translate into broad-based social change sensitive to intersectional vectors of social power? Can these legal victories address the ills of a carceral system embroiled in virulent racism, homophobia, transphobia, and misogyny—or do the victories mask these problems by upholding and valorizing that system?

As these questions emerge, the work of #MeToo/MeToo, in its conjoined configuration, becomes clearer.

The anti-rape movement must seek answers to these questions by developing an intersectional ethics for activism. It needs to draw on emerging visions of liberatory practices of justice, embracing the energy and brilliance of people who are developing critiques of the carceral system and positing better solutions for just outcomes. "Justice looks different for everyone and survivors don't think punitively," Tarana Burke has observed. "We want healing."[56]

Criticisms of #MeToo/MeToo are necessary and revelatory. The emerging discussions around legal and carceral outcomes of sexual assault reports reveal the institutionalization of sexual violence in systems supposedly set up to remedy that very problem. They also raise questions about whether legal and carceral solutions to sexual violence can actually advance the goal of creating a more just and humane world.

The real work of #MeToo/MeToo now is to imagine a world free of sexual abuse and violence, including institutional sexual violence, and to forge brave new models for creating it.

Coda
Reformulating Desire and Consent

As most people now know, "me too" was a motto that the African American feminist activist Tarana Burke created in order to encourage survivors of sexual violence in communities of color to share their experiences. The phrase was intentionally geared to creating a sisterhood of support; it was meant to provide strength and solace to girls and young women who had experienced sexual violence, letting them know that they were not alone. #MeToo picked up on and amplified Burke's work, using social media as a space where survivors could express the realities of sexual violence in their lives and, in speaking out, find solidarity with others.

Sexual violence, and rape in particular, is embodied assault; it involves the forcible invasion or penetration of a person's body by someone else. It is physically and psychically painful. It causes trauma to the body and to the spirit. #MeToo/MeToo remind us that so many people, especially women, experience this violence and the consequent trauma that rape must be seen, at a societal level, as "a structured phenomenon that produces specific material effects at the level of the body."[1]

To think of it this way is to see it as an "apparatus," to use a Foucauldian concept that has been taken up in feminist analysis. In Foucault's formulation, an apparatus (*dispositif*) refers not to a machine, but to a social formation that "has a dominant strategic function."[2] Rape and other forms of sexual violence have a strategic function in that they are used to dominate and terrorize certain categories of people, especially women; to exploit their socially imposed vulnerability in order to consolidate their subordinate status and at the same time reassert the power of others, too often male. The feminist scholar Carine Mardorossian points out that vulnerability is a human characteristic, "a function of human beings' permeability to others,"[3] not a weakness to be derided or exploited. Yet rape seizes on and intensifies existing vulnerabilities created by gender, race, class, disability, immigrant status, and other classifications.

To consider sexual violence as a social apparatus is to recognize the way it has figured in histories of colonization, slavery, genocide, racism, homophobia, and gender-based oppression, as well as the way it continues to shape our lives in workplaces, churches, colleges and schools, sports organizations, and homes. Sexual violence is so widespread and so entrenched in so many societies, in so many spaces and places, in so many cultures and conditions, that it is a defining feature of human life. It is not just about a chance encounter between a victim and an assailant. It is an enactment, at the individual level, of historically rooted social beliefs and structures that recode sex as violence and dehumanize people through sexual victimization. This recoding changes sex from an act that has the potential to be ethical—as well as playful, pleasurable, intimate, and loving—into an atrocity. As in the case of genocide, the resulting trauma affects society as well as the individual victim or survivor.

In the apparatus of sexual violence, the media are central mechanisms: they report on incidents of sexual violence, on reactions to them, on the statements made by various stakeholders; they are the cradle of commentaries, crossfire, rhetorical salvos, hashtags; they are the site of representations of sexual violence, both fictive and nonfictional. They have also been the site of silencing and discounting rape and its survivor victims. There are frictions involved in all this; but frictions create sparks. These mediated altercations are provoking intensive reflection as well as action.

A sharp critique of #MeToo—and of the MeToo movement, despite Tarana Burke's unwavering focus on marginalized communities—has been its overall description as a sanctum for privileged white women. The feminist scholar Alison Phipps describes #MeToo as embodying "political whiteness." #MeToo's feminism, she observes, "is nominally inclusive, but inclusion depends on white women being centered as those who grant it."[4] Indeed, this criticism of #MeToo surfaced almost immediately after Alyssa Milano's 2017 tweet: first it called attention to Tarana Burke as the originator of the hashtag and of the movement, then quickly prompted the formation of a separate hashtag, #WOCAffirmation, which was designed to articulate the experiences of women of color. These criticisms and reactions are crucial: they spur the interrogation of anti-rape activism and of its complex relationships with race and nation, border politics, class, gender and sexual orientation, disability, and religion.

The fact that #MeToo has resonated globally is important as well. Just a month after the hashtag appeared on Twitter, CNN reported 2.3 million #MeToo tweets from 85 countries. Feminist solidarity around rape and rape culture has been the motivating force behind the movement's worldwide resonance. "[I]t's for the first time in our history as women that we can speak the same language of sorrow and despair and of subordination," as the Romanian activist Andreea Molocea put it.[5] There is evidence that sharing experiences of sexual assault and harassment through social media has been a lifeline for women as well as for people of other genders. In China, for example, rape culture has flourished for years through the official and cultural repression of the realities of rape; but the recent emergence of "Wo Ye Shi" (the Chinese version of #MeToo) has raised women's consciousness about sexual violence and provided an outlet where survivors can "reveal their hidden pain from the past,"[6] as the gender scholars Zhongxuan Lin and Liu Yang explained.

In Pakistan, despite the real dangers of coming forward, more and more people share their stories online: "From sexual abuse suffered during childhood to public groping, thread after thread [has] reflected on personal trauma and societal denial of it," reports Al Jazeera columnist Rabia Mehmood, noting the need for survivors to "claim a space" in a hostile environment.[7] Not only have Pakistani women felt increasingly empowered to speak about sexual abuse and assault, but "#MeToo has opened the door to publicly acknowledging the issue of male rape in Pakistan, a taboo despite the alarming rate of crimes against young boys across the country."[8]

The Brazilian feminist scholar Raquel Paiva asserts that the MeToo movement in Brazil has had an unprecedented impact: "This is because the uncountable collectives, hashtags, and Facebook groups have mobilized generations of women, suggesting that a fourth-wave feminism is in course in the country."[9] She is optimistic about the potential for collective anti-rape action and pro-feminist transformation as a result of the conversations, which are drawing active participation from people, especially women, from diverse backgrounds and class positions.

These are just a few examples; it would be impossible to capture here easily the varied and complicated ways in which the MeToo movement has played out in different countries and cultures—but it is vitally important to recognize its global resonance and its validation of sexual violence as deeply embedded in women's and many others' lives. Although online activism around rape preexisted #MeToo, the catalytic effect of #MeToo/MeToo lies in the worldwide solidarity it has forged among survivors of sexual violence, as well as in the breaking of long-held silences.

To recognize this is not to blithely ignore the limitations

of hashtag feminism. The ability to participate in online conversations, even in regional languages, calls for both literacy and access to computers or cellphones, which disqualifies people who don't have the benefits of education, technology, and leisure time. Online sharing of sexual assault stories is not without its perils, either: trolling, victim blaming, and harassment of survivors are common.

In addition, in many political climates, the social and institutional backlash against anti-rape movements and survivors can be harsh. In fact the very reason for challenging rape culture is the recognition that it is so deeply enmeshed in systems of politics, law enforcement, jurisprudence, education, health care, and family life. In a recent study, Bangladeshi women expressed support of the #MeToo movement and its aims but felt that cultural and family pressures restrained them from disclosing their stories online; they were also held back by the fact that, as a 23-year-old student said, "[i]n Bangladesh, neither the society nor the police will help you. So, all you will bring for you is additional shame if you share your harassment online in public."[10] She believed that the western context was different—but, as we know, rape culture creates barriers for survivors everywhere when it comes to getting support and help. Despite these setbacks and obstacles, anti-rape activism persists, both online and offline.[11]

To recognize rape culture today is to recognize the way in which intersectional workings of power *position* some people as sexually vulnerable, others as sexually predatory. Rape does not happen because a person walked down a dark alley or wore a revealing outfit or did not have legal documentation. Rape happens because predators have been empowered in societies to interpret sex as a method of dominance and exploitation, and to do so with relative impunity.

This leads to the question of perpetrators and their accountability. If sexual assailants are structurally positioned as sexual assailants, are they responsible for their actions or are they not? To paraphrase the indie film *Repo Man*, did society make them do it?

Answering these questions is far from simple. Of course, in a very basic sense, there would be no rape if there were no rapists. And, indeed, human societies have existed where rape was rare if not nonexistent, which challenges the simplistic idea that rape correlates with some kind of biological instinct. In most contemporary societies, though, sexual violence is prevalent but, paradoxically, perpetrators are viewed as isolated villains: the social systems that enable them, and the ripple effects of rape, tend not to be addressed in our formal conventions. We focus on punishing specific individuals and we consider the job done. This focus has driven the media coverage of #MeToo, which is understandable: since news values prioritize both celebrity lives and criminality, the combination is bound to be irresistible media fodder.

Of course, prosecutions do have some value. The legal proceedings that led to the incarceration of Harvey Weinstein, Bill Cosby, and others were significant in that they validated women's accounts of sexual assault and confirmed the harm done by sexual abusers. These trials were also notable because health professionals with expertise in sexual violence were asked to testify and explain rape myths, post-rape trauma, and a whole range of survivors' reactions.[12] Survivor testimony was crucial to the proceedings, and all these procedural innovations helped disseminate information about sexual violence that had been shaped by feminist activism and scholarship. But the sentencing of these men was separate from any examination of workplace and social climates. The "monsters" were jailed, while the circumstances that created and abetted them were left intact. The cases also touched off a trend in which other men were publicly "named and shamed," which led to their dismissal, mainly from high-profile media jobs; and this in turn unleashed accusations of a "MeToo witch hunt."

This disparagement of anti-rape activism has triggered male backlash in the workplace that is damaging to women on multiple fronts and has its own silencing effects. The apocryphal "witch hunt" has caused a number of men to deliberately exclude female colleagues from professional activities, for fear of being falsely accused of sexual misconduct. Research shows that significant numbers of men are now "reluctant to hire attractive women," "reluctant to hire women for jobs involving close interpersonal interaction with men (such as travel)," and reluctant to have "one-on-one meetings with female colleagues."[13] Research also reveals that male hostility toward women in the workplace has risen after #MeToo, even though overt sexual harassment has declined.[14] "Most of the reaction to #MeToo was celebratory; it assumed women were really going to benefit," management professor Leanne Atwater told the *Harvard Business Review*.[15] But the backlash has been spiteful, a retaliation to an imagined threat of false sexual assault claims from women.

The real threat of MeToo is not a spate of false reports, which are very uncommon. Rather the threat is to predators' prerogative to abuse women sexually, in the workplace and elsewhere. "Women who dare to break the customary feminine silence about gender violence are often reminded there is a price to pay for their boldness," writes the masculinity scholar Jackson Katz. "They certainly run the risk of evoking men's hostility and anger, because to challenge men's right to control women is to threaten men who see such control as their birthright."[16] (He points out that women, too, can turn on other women who report sexual violence.)

The upshot of the popular media's focus on perpetrators and punishment is that the goals of progressive collective activism and societal healing have been sidelined by gender warfare, with inordinate psychic costs for everyone involved. Penalties are intended to be deterrents, and they may be; but they also seem to be making many men afraid of being allies in the movement to end sexual violence. Imposing penalties *after* sexual violence has been committed, writes Katz, "is essentially an admission of failure."[17] In order to address the social and cultural forces at work in sexual violence, we need proactive collective action. People of all genders, particularly men, are essential to changing a rape culture. It is crucial at this moment to open up more conversations about confronting sexual abuse, assault, and harassment; to think about how social justice can unfold in a way that acknowledges survivors' rights and needs while dispelling men's anxieties and including them as allies; and to emphasize our collective responsibility to end sexual violence.

The problems that have surfaced don't mean that #MeToo has failed: they mean only that the conversation has to continue. Resistance must be directed against rape culture, not against trusting relationships between people of all genders.

Three years in, it is really too early to gauge how effectively MeToo/#MeToo might fulfill its promise of a feminist transformation of our world into one free of sexual violence. Its potential at this very moment lies in unleashing a global and radically intersectional imagination. The social anthropologist Arjun Appadurai sees imagination as a central force in the world, "a staging ground for action."[18] Through a shared imagination inspired by mediated communication, communities are formed that are "often transnational, even postnational, and they frequently operate beyond the boundaries of the nation."[19] For Appadurai, a shared imagination can move such communities to collective action for radical change.

The current MeToo moment is a time for imagining—or perhaps reimagining. It is opening up ways of understanding sexual violence that speak to how rape culture affects us all, even those of us who are not survivors. Rape culture can't be simply defined, and this calls for imagination. Sexual violence takes different forms, and the context in which it occurs defines its impact and meaning. "[T]here should not be an assumption of a single, universally experienced and imposed wrong of rape," writes the philosopher Ann Cahill. "The phenomenon of rape will, it may be assumed, itself be differentiated not only by sex but by other factors of personhood."[20] And yet everyone who is a victim-survivor of sexual violence experiences a profound violation, a bodily invasion, a crime. This is the basis for a shared understanding and vision for change—in fact, a shared imagination.

The work of imagining is still in flux. The ability of survivors to articulate their lived experiences and to use them to create social and global change is new; it is the unexpected breakthrough of the MeToo movement. But the work has only just begun, and the varied reactions, criticisms, challenges, and defenses of MeToo are part of an unfolding process. We are in the midst of intense reflection on rape culture and its implications. This reflection is centered on survivors' stories, which raises another issue that haunts the anxieties around the MeToo movement: vulnerability. The place of vulnerability in many cultures, especially contemporary US culture, is perilous. MeToo and its entailments force a reckoning with vulnerability that has transformative potential.

A person who has experienced sexual violence has had to confront vulnerability; in speaking as a survivor, that person reveals a profound vulnerability. To say "me too" as a survivor is to share the feelings of exposure and helplessness that arise from being utterly vulnerable to a sexual attack. This is not a failing or a fault. People frequently find themselves in vulnerable circumstances. Carine Mardorossian observes that our very interdependence as humans renders us vulnerable to one another. "Rather than blame victims," she writes, "we should recognize that the crime of rape is the radical abuse of this fundamentally human condition."[21]

The MeToo movement finds strength in the shared recognition of vulnerability and its abuse. Vulnerability is the actual grounding of this fledgling social movement. When survivors say "me too," they mean that they, too, were vulnerable, in body and spirit, and they no longer want to construe that as a shameful secret. Instead, their vulnerability, and the open acknowledgment of it, is the starting point of healing and change.

Feminist media activism has a history of "reformulation," as the scholars Carolyn Byerly and Marcus Hill describe it. They argue that "feminist political activity serves to reframe (i.e. reformulate) the social meanings of women's experiences in women's own terminology."[22] Now, in the wake of #MeToo/MeToo, survivors' shared experiences are cutting through the fog of dubious concepts such as "nondisclosure," "consent," "slut," and "victim." Their voices mobilize ideas that are meant to change sexual cultures in order to change the dynamics of vulnerability—to advocate for sexual safety, to resist and halt predation. These insights come with the clear understanding that sexual violence is systemic and structural violence. To end sexual violence, it is essential to confront the realities of rape culture. And, as communities of healing and resistance emerge from these shared experiences, they are engaging with the imperatives and intricacies of diversity and inclusion.

These are ideas, but they are not mere abstractions. They address the variously embodied injuries of sexual violence, as well as their silencing by the interlocking systems of power that cause such injuries. They are not without peril. Yet the way these ideas generate reflections about collectivity, intersectionality, and activism bodes a paradigm shift. "Without imaginations (or embodiments) of alterity," asks the feminist philosopher Susan Bordo, "from what vantage point can we seek transformation of culture? And how will we construct these imaginations and embodiments, if not through alliance with that which has been silenced, repressed, disdained?"[23]

In our global reckoning with this MeToo moment and its confrontation with rape culture, we are seeking this vantage point, this silence-breaking work. Crucially, there is, among survivors and their allies, a growing hunger for clarity about truly assenting and welcome sex, in all its varied formations and figurations.

Notes

Notes to Introduction

1 Tarana Burke's nonprofit organization "Just Be" has trademarked the phrase as me too™, yet it is also widely used as a common expression, and the media version is frequently MeToo. #MeToo is the Twitter hashtag launched by the actor Alyssa Milano in 2017, amplifying Burke's previous activism around sexual violence.
2 Ohlheiser 2018. See also Fox and Diehm 2017; Dalvin Brown 2018.
3 Buchwald, Fletcher, and Roth 2005: 5.
4 Griffin 1971: 27.
5 Onwuachi-Willig 2018: 107.
6 Herman 1984: 45–6.
7 Russo 2001: 7.
8 Crenshaw 1991: 1241.
9 Ibid.
10 Russo 2001: 12.
11 Burt 1980: 217, 218.

12 See e.g. Barn and Powers 2018; Burt 1980; Edwards et al. 2011; Franiuk, Seefelt, and Vandello 2008; Haywood and Swank 2008: 373–89; Lonsway and Fitzgerald 1994; Ryan 2011.
13 See the definition of rape in FBI 2013.
14 Castañeda 1998: 317.
15 Jacquet 2019; Mallory, Hasenbush, and Sears 2015; Spohn and Tellis 2012.
16 Morgan and Oudekerk 2018; World Health Organization 2012.
17 Foucault 1980: 194–5.
18 Woodhull 1988: 168.
19 Kellner 1995: 42.
20 Zacharek, Dockterman, and Edwards 2017: 45.
21 Freire 1998: 478.
22 Kelly 1988: 163.
23 Utt 2014.
24 Kelly 1988: 76.
25 Crenshaw 1991: 1245.
26 Human Rights Campaign and Trans People of Color Coalition 2017.

Notes to Chapter 1

1 Chocano 2017: 12.
2 McGowan 2018: 116.
3 Hayek 2017.
4 Naff 2014.
5 Gilmore 2009: 4.
6 Gilmore 2009: 12.
7 Wolf 1991. Naomi Wolf notes that all professions

in which women develop a strong presence have become "display professions."

8 NBC News 2018.
9 Brownmiller 1975: 14.
10 MacKinnon 2016.
11 United Nations 2006.
12 Searles and Berger 1995: 2.
13 Katz 2006: 9.
14 Blumell and Sternadori 2018: 10.
15 Byerly 2011.
16 Lauzen 2018.
17 Quoted in Dowd 2017.
18 Uggens and Blackston 2004: 68.
19 Betzig 1995: 183.
20 Letourneau 1891: 49.
21 Harvey and Martinko 2009: 459.
22 Snow, Kern, and Curlette 2001: 104.
23 Rosenblatt 2012: 238.
24 Babiak, Neumann, and Hare 2010; Board and Fritzon 2005.
25 Smith and Lilienfeld 2013: 214.
26 Jacobs 2020.
27 Truman, Tokar, and Fischer 1996.
28 Stoltenberg 1989: 17.
29 Gilbert 1992: 391.
30 Hanson, Gizzarelli, and Scott 1994: 189.
31 See Hill and Fischer 2001.
32 Kimmel 2005: 14.
33 MacKinnon 1979: 217–18.
34 Usborne 2018: 106.
35 Hayes and Chmielewski 2018.
36 Calamur 2017.
37 Farrow 2018.

38 Mundy 2012; Terkel 2016.
39 Trotter 2013.
40 Dockterman 2019.
41 McGowan 2018: 8.
42 Farrow 2018: 47.
43 Feidelson 2020: 45.
44 Farrow 2018: 54.
45 Amy-Chinn 2006: 165.
46 Berger 1972: 47.
47 MacKinnon 1979: 21.
48 MacKinnon 1979: 23.
49 Crockett 2016.
50 Malone 2015; see also Mallenbaum, Ryan, and Puente 2018.
51 Savage 2019.
52 Sherman 2016.
53 Farrow 2018.
54 Levine and Hod 2017.
55 Kantor and Twohey 2017: A1.
56 Bowman 2014.
57 Schmidt, Rodgers, and Cuttino 2018.
58 Bravo 2018.
59 Hayek 2017.
60 Nyong'o 2017.
61 Farrow 2017a.
62 Desta 2017.
63 Farrow 2018.
64 Zacharek, Dockterman, and Edwards 2017: 36.
65 Jones 2014: 56.
66 Haraway 1991: 304.
67 See e.g. Buchwald, Fletcher, and Roth 2005; Harding 2015; Herman 1984; Phillips 2017.
68 Lucero 2015: 5.

69 Brummett 1980: 289.
70 Prasad 2018: 2509.
71 Abrams and Koblin 2018.
72 Edgers 2018.
73 Derogatis and Pallasch 2000: 14.
74 Farrow 2019: 108.
75 Donovan 2014; Kingston 2014.
76 Farrow 2017b.
77 Grove 2020.
78 Gross 2019a; North 2019; Palazzolo, Rothfeld, and Alpert 2016.
79 Swaine 2018.
80 National Sexual Violence Resource Center 2012.
81 Kantor and Twohey 2017.
82 Snider 2017.
83 Stanglin 2017.
84 Kirby 2018a.
85 Belton 2014.
86 Derogatis and Pallasch 2000; Edgers 2018.
87 Chiu 2019.
88 Osipova and Melas 2020.
89 Connell 1987: 81.
90 Prasad 2018: 2521.
91 Prasad 2018: 2537.
92 Pilon 2019: 89.
93 Cocks 1989: 44–5.
94 Cahill 2001: 3.
95 Gavey 2005: 70.
96 Gavey 2005: 71.
97 Roth 2017: 79.
98 Cohen 1995: 89.
99 Fahrenthold 2018.
100 Fahrenthold 2018: minute 0:15–0:29.

101 Fahrenthold 2018: minute 1:16–1:28.
102 Fahrenthold 2018: para. 21.
103 Harp 2018.
104 Harp 2018: 203.
105 Foucault 1990: 11.
106 Stockton 2017: 174.
107 Buchwald, Fletcher, and Roth 2005: xi.
108 Lind 2016.
109 Filipovic 2017.
110 Schwartz, Caprara, and Vecchione 2010: 421–52.
111 Ceccarelli 2011.
112 Castaldo 2013.
113 Beinart 2019 (for both quotations).
114 See Mao 2019.
115 Saner 2013.
116 Bienkov 2019.
117 Kitroeff 2020: 17.
118 Kellner 1995: 3.
119 The Pussyhat Project 2020.
120 Paulins et al. 2017: 74.
121 Paulins et al. 2017.
122 Larabee 2017: 216. It is also important to note here that a statement on the Pussyhat Project's website explains that the color of the hat was chosen because of its association with femininity and was never intended to represent any particular person's anatomy (see https://www.pussyhatproject.com/faq).
123 Sanders 2018: 7.
124 North 2020.
125 Global Fund for Women n.d.
126 Stockman 2018.
127 Brewer and Dundes 2018.
128 Armstrong 1994: 206.

Notes to Chapter 2

1 Feimster 2015: 251.
2 Feimster 2015: 252.
3 Feimster 2015: 253–4.
4 Feimster 2015: 254.
5 Davis 1983: 29.
6 Feimster 2009.
7 McGuire 2010: xvii.
8 McGuire 2010: xix.
9 Murray 2017. This item, formerly at https://www.bet.com/celebrities/news/2017/12/07/tarana-burke.html, is no longer available.
10 *TIME* 2019.
11 Rezack 1998: 59.
12 Deer 2015: x, xi.
13 Martin 2019.
14 First Peoples Worldwide 2020.
15 Weaver 2009: 1557.
16 Deer 2015: 20.
17 Todorov 1999: 49.
18 MacGillivray 2016: 1.
19 Duncan 2004: 48.
20 Yung 1995: 33.
21 Duffett 1970: 570–1.
22 Weaver 2012: 46.
23 Matthews 2005: 106.
24 Human Rights Watch 2012.
25 Human Rights Watch 2012.
26 Time's Up 2020.
27 Russo 2001: 18.
28 Couric 2018.
29 Stein 2012: 80.

30 Currah 2008: 95.
31 Currah 2008: 96.
32 Taylor and Rupp 1993: 45.
33 Basile, Breiding, and Smith 2016; Harrell 2017; Scherer and Reyns 2019.
34 Shapiro 2018.
35 Abramson 2010.
36 @GeorgesDryad, Twitter, February 21, 2018 (visit https://twitter.com/DisVisibility/status/966465561470251008).
37 @CallaLily57, Twitter, February 21, 2018 (visit https://twitter.com/DisVisibility/status/966465561470251008).
38 Rooted in Rights 2018.
39 Smith et al. 2017.
40 Lowe and Rogers 2017: 40.
41 Guadalupe-Diaz 2015: 178.
42 Trombino and Funk 2019: 45.
43 @ScottyKirk75, #MeTooMen, December 3, 2018 (visit https://twitter.com/search?q=%23MeTooMen&src=typed_query&f=live).
44 Stone and Vogelstein 2019.
45 Lilla 2016.
46 Dyer 2002: 83.
47 Editors of the *Cahiers du Cinema* 1972: 8.
48 *Monitor* 2014. This article, published on November 4 and titled "Desire Luzinda should be locked up and isolated," is no longer available at https://www.monitor.co.ug/News/National/Desire-Luzinda-should-be-locked-up-and-isolated--Lokodo/688334-2510248-e7ukrg/index.html.
49 Chisala-Tempelhoff and Kirya 2016.
50 Scaptura and Boyle 2020.

51 Buni and Chemaly 2014.
52 Citron 2014; Pew Research Center 2017.
53 Citron 2014: 196.
54 Jane 2014.
55 Byaruhanga 2014.
56 Citron 2015.
57 Dean 2012.
58 Downing et al. 2017; Foubert, Brosi, and Bannon 2011.
59 Grosz 1994: 60.
60 Berger 1972: 55.
61 Ward, Merriwether, and Caruthers 2006: 703.
62 Doane 1982: 85.
63 Fuss 1992: 713.
64 Nurik 2018: 537.
65 Nurik 2018: 537.
66 Nurik 2018: 537.
67 Foubert et al. 2019.
68 Bridges et al. 2010.
69 Gorman, Monk-Turner, and Fish 2010.
70 Eck 2001: 604.
71 Buchwald, Fletcher, and Roth 2005: xi.
72 Vitis and Gilmour 2016.
73 Citron 2014: 20.
74 Keller, Mendes, and Ringrose 2018.
75 Keller, Mendes, and Ringrose 2018: 33.
76 Stuart 2019.
77 Clark-Parsons 2019: 5.
78 Reilly 2019: 10.
79 Kirby 2018b.
80 Valenti 2013.
81 Perloff 2000: 320.
82 Perloff 2000: 322.

83 Soderlund 2002: 453.
84 Soderlund 2002: 439.
85 Malone 1999: 49.
86 Gorham 1978: 353.
87 Gorham 1978: 375.
88 Gil de Zúñiga and Hinsley 2013: 927.
89 Ardovini-Brooker and Caringella-MacDonald 2002; Barca 2018; Benedict 1992; Caputi 1987; Carter 1998; Clark 1992; Cuklanz 1996; Durham 2013; Meyers 1997; Nava 1988; Stanko 1990; Taylor 2009.
90 Meyers 1997: 103.
91 McKinney 2006.
92 Wykes 1998.
93 Benedict 1992.
94 Cacciola and Mather 2018.
95 Edmonson and Tracy 2018.
96 Thenappan 2020.
97 *Miami Herald* and McClatchy Newspapers 2019.
98 Larson 2015.
99 Larson 2015.
100 Julie K. Brown 2018.
101 Julie K. Brown 2018.
102 Deitsch 2018.
103 Coronel, Coll, and Kravitz 2015.
104 Gross 2019b.
105 Deitsch 2018.
106 Pollitt 1995: 27.
107 Smith et al. 2017: 20.
108 Jacobs 2019.
109 Tillman et al. 2010: 64.
110 Asian Pacific Institute on Gender-Based Violence 2018.

111 Amnesty International 2006.
112 Zadnik and Melendez 2014.
113 Office for Victims of Crime 2014.
114 Stotzer 2009.
115 Walker 2011: 93.

Notes to Chapter 3

1 *New York Daily Times* 1851: 2.
2 Beeson 2018.
3 Kaminer 2018.
4 Kersten 2019.
5 Way 2018.
6 Flanagan 2018.
7 Flanagan 2018.
8 Gavey 2005: 123.
9 Way 2018.
10 Gavey 2005: 128.
11 Way 2018.
12 Butler 1999: 173.
13 Butler 1999: 178.
14 Edwards et al. 2011: 765.
15 Basow and Minieri 2011.
16 Fisher et al. 2007: 29.
17 Brison 2002: 6–7.
18 Cahill 2001: 3.
19 MacKinnon 2016: 450.
20 National Sexual Violence Resource Center 2012.
21 Linskey and Sullivan 2020.
22 Marotta 2018.
23 Gavey 2005: 64.
24 Katz 2006: 270.

25 Hsu 2019: 270.
26 Grady 2020.
27 Brison 2002: 18.
28 Mallenbaum, Ryan, and Puente 2018.
29 France 2020.
30 Farrow 2020.
31 Taylor 2019: 1.
32 Zamalin 2017: 120.
33 Schoenfeld 2018: 11.
34 Ross-Pilkington 2017.
35 Colon et al. 2018.
36 Stacey, Martin, and Brick 2017: 229.
37 Stacey, Martin, and Brick 2017: 229.
38 Guadalupe-Diaz 2015: 178; Russo 2001: 18.
39 Hsu 2019: 279.
40 Broadus 2009: 561.
41 Broadus 2009: 570.
42 Clayworth 2018.
43 Time's Up 2020.
44 Bernstein 2010.
45 2018: 99.
46 Davis 2003: 10.
47 Taylor 2019: 3.
48 Taylor 2018: 29.
49 Hsu 2019: 283.
50 INCITE! n.d.
51 Katz 2006: 117.
52 See Rentschler 2017.
53 Musto 2019: 39.
54 Backhouse 2012: 734.
55 Burke 2018.
56 Uribe and Yu 2020.

Notes to Coda

1 Balsamo 1996: 159.
2 Foucault 1980: 195.
3 Mardorossian 2014: 15.
4 Phipps 2019.
5 Radu 2017.
6 Lin and Yang 2019: 119.
7 Mehmood 2018.
8 Rashid 2019.
9 Paiva 2019: 241.
10 Hassan et al. 2019: 4.
11 Mendes, Ringrose, and Keller 2018.
12 Francescani 2020.
13 Bower 2019.
14 Johnson et al. 2019.
15 *Harvard Business Review* 2019.
16 Katz 2006: 73.
17 Katz 2006: 7.
18 Appadurai 1996: 31.
19 Appadurai 1996: 8.
20 Cahill 2001: 191.
21 Mardorossian 2014: 130–1.
22 Byerly and Hill 2012: 17.
23 Bordo 1993: 41.

References

Abrams, Rachel and John Koblin. 2018. "CBS paid the actress Eliza Dushku $9.5 million to settle harassment claims." *New York Times*, December 13. https://www.nytimes.com/2018/12/13/business/media/cbs-bull-weatherly-dushku-sexual-harassment.html.

Abramson, Wendie H. 2010. *Supporting Sexual Assault Survivors with Disabilities*. Sacramento: California Coalition against Sexual Assault. https://www.calcasa.org/wp-content/uploads/2010/12/Survivors-with-Disabilities.pdf.

Ahmed, Sara. 2016. *Living a Feminist Life*. Durham, NC: Duke University Press.

Amnesty International. 2006. *Maze of Injustice*. New York: Amnesty International. https://www.amnestyusa.org/reports/maze-of-injustice.

Amy-Chinn, Dee. 2006. "This is just for me(n): How the regulation of post-feminist lingerie advertising perpetuates woman as object." *Journal of Consumer Culture* 6(2): 155–75.

Appadurai, Arjun. 1996. *Modernity at Large: Cultural*

Dimensions of Globalization. Minneapolis: University of Minnesota Press.

Ardovini-Brooker, Joanne and Susan Caringella-MacDonald. 2002. "Media attributions of blame and sympathy in ten rape cases." *Justice Professional* 15(1): 3–18.

Armstrong, Louise. 1994. *Rocking the Cradle of Sexual Politics*. Reading, MA: Addison-Wesley.

Asian Pacific Institute on Gender-Based Violence. 2018. *Fact Sheet: Sexual Violence in Asian and Pacific Islander Communities*. Oakland, CA: API-GBV.

Babiak, Paul, Craig S. Neumann, and Robert D. Hare. 2010. "Corporate psychopathy: Talking the walk." *Behavioral Sciences & the Law* 28(2): 174–93.

Backhouse, Constance. 2012. "A feminist remedy for sexual assault: A quest for answers." In *Sexual Assault in Canada: Law, Legal Practice, and Women's Activism*, edited by Elizabeth A. Sheehy. Ottawa: University of Ottawa Press, pp. 725–40.

Balsamo, Anne. 1996. *Technologies of the Gendered Body: Reading Cyborg Women*. Durham, NC: Duke University Press.

Barca, Lisa A. 2018. "The agency factor: Neoliberal configurations of risk in news discourse on the Steubenville, Ohio rape case." *Critical Discourse Studies* 15(3): 265–84.

Barn, Ravinder and Ráchael A. Powers. 2018. "Rape myth acceptance in contemporary times: A comparative study of university students in India and the United Kingdom." *Journal of Interpersonal Violence*. doi: 10.1177/0886260518775750.

Basile, Kathleen C., Matthew J. Breiding, and Sharon G. Smith. 2016. "Disability and risk of recent sexual violence in the United States." *American Journal of Public Health* 106(5): 928–33.

Basow, Susan A. and Alexandra Minieri. 2011. "'You owe me:' Effects of date cost, who pays, participant gender, and rape myth beliefs on perceptions of rape." *Journal of Interpersonal Violence* 26(3): 479–97.

Beeson, Katie Packer. 2018. "Has #MeToo gone too far?" *US News & World Report*, February 12. https://www.usnews.com/opinion/civil-wars/articles/2018-02-12/metoo-movement-shouldnt-be-exploited-to-ruin-mens-careers-without-cause.

Beinart, Peter. 2019. "The new authoritarians are waging war on women." *The Atlantic*, January/February. https://www.theatlantic.com/magazine/archive/2019/01/authoritarian-sexism-trump-duterte/576382.

Belton, Danielle C. 2014. "Bill Cosby: Comedian, philanthropist, but rape allegations won't go away." *The Root*, November 11. https://www.theroot.com/bill-cosby-comedian-philanthropist-but-rape-allegati-1790877676.

Benedict, Helen. 1992. *Virgin or Vamp: How the Press Covers Sex Crimes*. New York: Oxford University Press.

Berger, John. 1972. *Ways of Seeing*. London: Penguin.

Bernstein, Elizabeth. 2010. "Militarized humanitarianism meets carceral feminism: the politics of sex, rights, and freedom in contemporary antitrafficking campaigns." *Signs: Journal of Women in Culture and Society* 36(1): 45–71.

Betzig, Laura. 1995. "Medieval monogamy." *Journal of Family History* 20(2): 181–216.

Bienkov, Adam. 2019. "Boris Johnson called gay men 'tank-topped bumboys' and black people 'picanninnies' with 'watermelon smiles.'" *Business Insider*, November 22. https://www.businessinsider.com/boris-johnson-record-sexist-homophobic-and-racist-comments-bumboys-piccaninnies-2019-6.

Blumell, Lindsey and Miglena Sternadori. 2018. "Godlike men and sex assault coverage: The cases of Kumar and Cosby." *Media Report to Women* 46(3): 6–11, 21–3.

Board, Belinda Jane and Katarina Fritzon. 2005. "Disordered personalities at work." *Psychology, Crime & Law* 11(1): 17–32.

Bordo, Susan. 1993. *Unbearable Weight: Feminism, Western Culture, and the Body*. Berkeley: University of California Press.

Bower, Tim. 2019. "The #MeToo backlash." *Harvard Business Review*, September–October. https://hbr.org/2019/09/the-metoo-backlash.

Bowman, Barbara. 2014. "Bill Cosby raped me: Why did it take 30 years for people to believe my story?" *Washington Post*, November 13. https://www.washingtonpost.com/posteverything/wp/2014/11/13/bill-cosby-raped-me-why-did-it-take-30-years-for-people-to-believe-my-story.

Bravo, Reah. 2018. "The open secret of Charlie Rose." *New York Review of Books*, May 4. https://www.nybooks.com/daily/2018/05/04/the-open-secret-of-charlie-rose.

Brewer, Sierra and Lauren Dundes. 2018. "Concerned, meet terrified: Intersectional feminism and the women's march." *Women's Studies International Forum* 69: 49–55.

Bridges, Ana J., Robert Wosnitzer, Erica Scharrer, Chyng Sun, and Rachael Liberman. 2010. "Aggression and sexual behavior in best-selling pornography videos: A content analysis update." *Violence Against Women* 16(10): 1065–85.

Brison, Susan. 2002. *Aftermath: Violence and the Remaking of a Self*. Princeton, NJ: Princeton University Press.

Broadus, Kylar W. 2009. "Intersections of transgender lives and the law: The criminal justice system and trans people." *Temple Political and Civil Rights Law Review* 18: 561–783.

Brown, Dalvin. 2018. "19 million tweets later: A look at #MeToo a year after the hashtag went viral." *USA Today*, October 13. https://www.usatoday.com/story/news/2018/10/13/metoo-impact-hashtag-made-online/1633570002.

Brown, Julie K. 2018. "How a future Trump Cabinet member gave a serial sex offender the deal of a lifetime." Perversion of Justice, Part I. *Miami Herald*, November 28. https://www.miamiherald.com/news/local/article220097825.html.

Brownmiller, Susan. 1975. *Against Our Will: Men, Women, and Rape*. New York: Simon & Schuster.

Brummett, Barry. 1980. "Towards a theory of silence as a political strategy." *Quarterly Journal of Speech* 66(3): 289–303.

Buchwald, Emilie, Pamela R. Fletcher, and Martha Roth. 2005. *Transforming a Rape Culture*. Minneapolis: Milkweed Editions.

Buni, Catherine and Soraya Chemaly. 2014. "The unsafety net: How social media turned against women." *The Atlantic*, October 9. https://www.theatlantic.com/technology/archive/2014/10/the-unsafety-net-how-social-media-turned-against-women/381261.

Burke, Tarana. 2018. "MeToo is a movement, not a moment." TED talk, November. https://www.ted.com/talks/tarana_burke_me_too_is_a_movement_not_a_moment?language=en.

Burt, Martha. 1980. "Cultural myths and supports for rape." *Journal of Personality and Social Psychology* 38(2): 217–30.

Butler, Judith. 1999. *Gender Trouble: Feminism and the Subversion of Identity*. New York: Routledge.

Byaruhanga, Catherine. 2014. "Ugandan 'revenge porn' victim could be arrested." BBC News, November 11. https://www.bbc.com/news/av/world-africa-30011166.

Byerly, Carolyn M. 2011. *Global Report on the Status of Women in the News Media*. Washington, DC: International Women's Media Foundation.

Byerly, Carolyn and Marcus Hill. 2012. "Reformulation theory: Gauging feminist impact on news of violence against women." *Journal of Research on Women and Gender* 5: 1–20.

Cacciola, Scott and Victor Mather. 2018. "Larry Nassar sentencing: 'I just signed your death warrant.'" *New York Times*, January 24. https://www.nytimes.com/2018/01/24/sports/larry-nassar-sentencing.html.

Cahill, Ann J. 2001. *Rethinking Rape*. Ithaca: Cornell University Press.

Calamur, Krishnadev. 2017. "Bill O'Reilly's exit from Fox News." *The Atlantic*, April 19. https://www.theatlantic.com/news/archive/2017/04/fox-fires-oreilly/523590.

Caputi, Jane. 1987. *The Age of Sex Crime*. London: Women's Press.

Carter, Cynthia. 1998. "When the 'extraordinary'

becomes 'ordinary': Everyday news of sexual violence." In *News, Gender and Power*, edited by Cynthia Carter, Gill Branston, and Stuart Allen. New York: Routledge, pp. 219–32.

Castaldo, Antonio. 2013. "Angelo Bruno, 'Ma che onorata, imbarazzata': Offesa da Berlusconi, 'Quante volte viene?'" *Corriere della Sera*, February 12. https://www.corriere.it/politica/speciali/2013/elezioni/notizie/12-febbraio-berlusconi-bruno_8f93f54c-74f1-11e2-b332-8f62ddea2ca4.shtml.

Castañeda, Antonia. 1998. "History and the politics of violence against women." In *Living Chicana Theory*, edited by Carla Trujillo. Berkeley: University of California Press, pp. 310–19.

Ceccarelli, Filipo. 2011. "Il Cavaliere lancia 'Forza Gnocca': Così l'ossessione diventa un partito." *La Repubblica*, October 7. https://www.repubblica.it/politica/2011/10/07/news/ossessione_cavaliere-22832716/index.html?ref=search.

Chisala-Tempelhoff, Sarai and Monica Twesiime Kirya. 2016. "Gender, law and revenge porn in Sub-Saharan Africa: A review of Malawi and Uganda." *Palgrave Communication* 2. https://doi.org/10.1057/palcomms.2016.69.

Chiu, Rowena. 2019. "Harvey Weinstein told me he liked Chinese girls." *New York Times*, October 5. https://www.nytimes.com/2019/10/05/opinion/sunday/harvey-weinstein-rowena-chiu.html.

Chocano, Carina. 2017. "Plain sight." *New York Times Magazine*, November 26.

Citron, Danielle Keats. 2014. *Hate Crimes in Cyberspace*. Cambridge, MA: Harvard University Press.

Citron, Danielle Keats. 2015. "Addressing cyber

harassment: An overview of hate crimes in cyberspace." *Journal of Law, Technology & the Internet* 6: 1–11.

Clark, Kate. 1992. "The linguistics of blame: Representations of women in *The Sun*'s reporting of crimes of sexual violence." In *Language, Text and Context: Essays in Stylistics*, edited by Michael Toolan. New York: Routledge, pp. 208–24.

Clark-Parsons, Rosemary. 2019. "'I SEE YOU, I BELIEVE YOU, I STAND WITH YOU': #MeToo and the performance of networked feminist visibility." *Feminist Media Studies*: 1–19. doi: 10.1080/14680777.2019.1628797.

Clayworth, Jason. 2018. "Capitol harassment: Lewd, intimidating conduct has created a 'toxic' statehouse, staffers and lawmakers say." *Des Moines Register*, October 14. https://www.desmoinesregister.com/story/news/investigations/2018/10/14/iowa-capitol-legislature-sexual-harassment-me-too-depositions-lawmakers-porn-senate-kirsten-anderson/1187425002.

Cocks, Joan. 1989. *The Oppositional Imagination: Feminism Critique and Political Theory*. New York: Routledge.

Cohen, Jeffrey E. 1995. "Presidential rhetoric and the public agenda." *American Journal of Political Science*: 87–107.

Colon, Katy M., Philip R. Kavanaugh, Don Hummer, and Eileen M. Ahlin. 2018. "The impact of race and extra-legal factors in charging defendants with serious sexual assault: Findings from a five-year study of one Pennsylvania court jurisdiction." *Journal of Ethnicity in Criminal Justice* 16(2): 99–116.

Connell, R. W. 1987. *Gender and Power*. Stanford, CA: Stanford University Press.

Coronel, Sheila, Steve Coll, and Derek Kravitz. 2015. "*Rolling Stone*'s investigation: 'A failure that was avoidable.'" *Columbia Journalism Review*, April 5. https://www.cjr.org/investigation/rolling_stone_investigation.php.

Couric, Katie. 2018. "Wonder woman: Laverne Cox: Next question with Katie Couric." Podcast audio, February 8. https://podcasts.apple.com/us/podcast/katie-couric/id1134154895?i=1000401752007&mt=2.

Crenshaw, Kimberlé Williams. 1991. "Mapping the margins: Intersectionality, identity politics, and violence against women of color." *Stanford Law Review* 43(6): 1241–99.

Crockett, Emily. 2016. "Here are the women who have publicly accused Roger Ailes of sexual harassment." *Vox*, August 15. https://www.vox.com/2016/8/15/12416662/roger-ailes-fox-sexual-harassment-women-list.

Cuklanz, Lisa. 1996. *Rape on Trial: How the Mass Media Construct Legal Reform and Social Change*. Philadelphia: University of Pennsylvania Press.

Currah, Paisley. 2008. "Stepping back, looking outward: Situating transgender activism and transgender studies: Kris Hayashi, Matt Richardson, and Susan Stryker frame the movement." *Sexuality Research & Social Policy* 5(1): 93–109.

Davis, Angela. 1983. *Women, Race and Class*. New York: Vintage.

Davis, Angela. 2003. *Are Prisons Obsolete?* New York: Seven Stories Press.

Dean, Michelle. 2012. "The story of Amanda Todd." *New Yorker*, October 18. https://www.newyorker.com/culture/culture-desk/the-story-of-amanda-todd.

Deer, Sarah. 2015. *The Beginning and End of Rape: Confronting Sexual Violence in Native America.* Minneapolis: University of Minnesota Press.

Deitsch, Richard. 2018. "Inside the reporting of five journalists that helped end Larry Nassar's serial sexual abuse." *Sports Illustrated*, February 7. https://www.si.com/media/2018/02/07/larry-nassar-investigation-sentencing-indy-star-media-reporters-roundtable.

Derogatis, Jim and Abdon M. Pallasch. 2000. "Kelly accused of sex with teenage girls." *Chicago Sun-Times*, December 14.

Desta, Yohana. 2017. "Graphic, disturbing details of Matt Lauer's alleged sexual misconduct." *Vanity Fair*, November 29. https://www.vanityfair.com/hollywood/2017/11/matt-lauer-sexual-misconduct-allegations.

Doane, Mary Ann. 1982. "Film and the masquerade: Theorising the female spectator." *Screen* 23(3–4): 74–88.

Dockterman, Eliana. 2019. "The true story behind *Bombshell* and the Fox News sexual harassment scandal." *TIME*, December 16. https://time.com/5748267/bombshell-true-story-fox-news.

Donovan, Kevin. 2014. "Jian Ghomeshi: 8 women accuse former CBC host of violence, sexual abuse, or harassment." *Toronto Star*, October 29. https://www.thestar.com/news/gta/2014/10/29/jian_ghomeshi_8_women_accuse_former_cbc_host_of_violence_sexual_abuse_or_harassment.html?li_source=LI&li_medium=star_web_ymbii.

Dowd, Maureen. 2017. "Harvey Weinstein, Hollywood's oldest horror story." *New York Times*, October 14. https://www.nytimes.com/2017/10/14/opinion/sunday/harvey-weinstein-dowd-hollywood.html?action=click&contentCollection=Opinion&module=RelatedCoverage®ion=EndOfArticle&pgtype=article.

Downing, Martin J., Eric W. Schrimshaw, Roberta Scheinmann, Nadav Antebi-Gruszka, and Sabina Hirshfield. 2017. "Sexually explicit media use by sexual identity: a comparative analysis of gay, bisexual, and heterosexual men in the United States." *Archives of Sexual Behavior* 46(6): 1763–76.

Duffett, John, ed. 1970. *Against the Crime of Silence: Proceedings from the International War Crimes Tribunal*. New York: Clarion Books.

Duncan, Patti. 2004. *Tell This Silence: Asian American Women Writers and the Politics of Speech*. Iowa City: University of Iowa Press.

Durham, Meenakshi Gigi. 2013. "'Vicious assault shakes Texas town': The politics of gender violence in *The New York Times*' coverage of a schoolgirl's gang rape." *Journalism Studies* 14(1): 1–12.

Dyer, Richard. 2002. *The Matter of Images: Essays on Representation*, 2d edn. New York: Routledge.

Eck, Beth A. 2001. "Nudity and framing: Classifying art, pornography, information, and ambiguity." *Sociological Forum* 16(4): 603–32.

Edgers, Geoff. 2018. "The star treatment." *Washington Post*, May 4. https://www.washingtonpost.com/news/style/wp/2018/05/04/feature/how-the-music-industry-overlooked-r-kellys-alleged-abuse-of-young-women.

The Editors of the *Cahiers du Cinema*. 1972. "John Ford's 'Young Mr. Lincoln.'" *Screen* 13(3): 5–45.

Edmonson, Catie and Mark Tracy. 2018. "'It can happen even to guys': Ohio state wrestlers detail abuse, saying #UsToo." *New York Times*, August 2. https://www.nytimes.com/2018/08/02/us/politics/ohio-state-wrestlers-abuse-me-too.html.

Edwards, Katie M., Jessica A. Turchik, Christina M. Dardis, Nicole Reynolds, and Christine A. Gidycz. 2011. "Rape myths: History, individual and institutional-level presence, and implications for change." *Sex Roles* 65(11/12): 761–73.

Fahrenthold, David A. 2018. "Trump recorded having extremely lewd conversation about women in 2005." *Washington Post*, October 8. https://www.washingtonpost.com/politics/trump-recorded-having-extremely-lewd-conversation-about-women-in-2005/2016/10/07/3b9ce776-8cb4-11e6-bf8a-3d26847eeed4_story.html.

Farrow, Ronan. 2017a. "From aggressive overtures to sexual assault: Harvey Weinstein's accusers tell their stories." *New Yorker*, October 23. https://www.newyorker.com/news/news-desk/from-aggressive-overtures-to-sexual-assault-harvey-weinsteins-accus ers-tell-their-stories.

Farrow, Ronan. 2017b. "Harvey Weinstein's secret settlements." *New Yorker*, November 21. https://www.newyorker.com/news/news-desk/harvey-weinsteins-secret-settlements.

Farrow, Ronan. 2018. "Les Moonves and CBS face allegations of sexual misconduct." *New Yorker*, July 27. https://www.newyorker.com/magazine/2018/08/06/

les-moonves-and-cbs-face-allegations-of-sexual-misconduct?reload.

Farrow, Ronan. 2019. *Catch and Kill: Lies, Spies, and a Conspiracy to Protect Predators*. New York: Little, Brown.

Farrow, Ronan. 2020. "'I haven't exhaled in so long': Surviving Harvey Weinstein." *New Yorker*, February 25.

FBI. 2013. *Crime in the United States, 2013*. FBI Uniform Crime Report. Washington, DC: US Department of Justice. https://ucr.fbi.gov/crime-in-the-u.s/2013/crime-in-the-u.s.-2013/violent-crime/rape.

Feidelson, Lizzie. 2020. "The sex choreographer." *New York Times Magazine*, January 19.

Feimster, Crystal. 2009. *Southern Horrors: Women And The Politics Of Rape And Lynching*. Cambridge, MA: Harvard University Press.

Feimster, Crystal. 2015. "'What if I am a woman?' Black women's campaigns for sexual justice and citizenship." In *The World the Civil War Made*, edited by Gregory P. Downs and Kate Masur. Chapel Hill, NC: University of North Carolina Press, pp. 249–68.

Filipovic, Jill. 2017. "Our president has always degraded women: And we've always let him." *TIME*, December 5. https://time.com/5047771/donald-trump-comments-billy-bush.

First Peoples Worldwide. 2020. "Violence from extractive industry 'man camps' endangers indigenous women and children." January 29. https://www.colorado.edu/program/fpw/2020/01/29/violence-extractive-industry-man-camps-endangers-indigenous-women-and-children.

Fisher, Bonnie S., Leah E. Daigle, Francis T. Cullen, and Shannon A. Santana. 2007. "Assessing the efficacy of the protective action–completion nexus for sexual victimizations." *Violence and Victims* 22(1): 18–42.

Flanagan, Caitlin. 2018. "The humiliation of Aziz Ansari." *The Atlantic*, January 14. https://www.theatlantic.com/entertainment/archive/2018/01/the-humiliation-of-aziz-ansari/550541.

Foubert, John D., Matthew W. Brosi, and R. Sean Bannon. 2011. "Pornography viewing among fraternity men: Effects on bystander intervention, rape myth acceptance and behavioral intent to commit sexual assault." *Sexual Addiction & Compulsivity* 18(4): 212–31.

Foubert, John D., Will Blanchard, Michael Houston, and Richard R. Williams, Jr. 2019. "Pornography and sexual violence." In *Handbook of Sexual Assault and Sexual Assault Prevention*, edited by William T. O'Donohue and Paul A. Schewe. Cham: Springer International Publishing, pp. 109–27.

Foucault, Michel. 1980. *Power/Knowledge: Selected Interviews and Other Writings, 1972–1977*, edited by Colin Gordon. New York: Pantheon Books.

Foucault, Michel. 1990. *The History of Sexuality: An Introduction*, vol. 1, translated by Robert Hurley. New York: Vintage.

Fox, Kara and Jan Diehm. 2017. "#MeToo's global moment: The anatomy of a viral campaign." CNN, November 9. https://www.cnn.com/2017/11/09/world/metoo-hashtag-global-movement/index.html.

France, Lisa Respers. 2020. "Ashley Judd, Rosanna Arquette and others react to Weinstein Verdict." CNN, February 25. https://www.google.com/search?

q=Lisa+Respers+France+Ashley+Judd&oq=Lisa+Respers+France+Ashley+Judd&aqs=chrome..69i57j33l2.7941j0j7&sourceid=chrome&ie=UTF-8.

Francescani, Chris. 2020. "Expert witness details 'rape myths' in Harvey Weinstein case." ABC News, January 24. https://abcnews.go.com/US/expert-witness-details-rape-myths-harvey-weinstein-case/story?id=68504135.

Franiuk, Renae, Jennifer L. Seefelt, and Joseph A. Vandello. 2008. "Prevalence of rape myths in headlines and their effects on attitudes toward rape." *Sex Roles* 58(11/12): 790–801.

Freire, Paulo. 1998. "Cultural action for freedom: Author's introduction." *Harvard Education Review* 68(4): 478–521.

Fuss, Diana. 1992. "Fashion and the homospectatorial look." *Critical Inquiry* 18(4): 713–37.

Gavey, Nicola. 2005. *Just Sex? The Cultural Scaffolding of Rape*. New York: Routledge.

Gil de Zúñiga, Homero and Amber Hinsley. 2013. "The press versus the public: What is 'good journalism?'" *Journalism Studies* 14(6): 926–42.

Gilbert, Lucia A. 1992. "Gender and counseling psychology: Current knowledge and directions for research and social action." In *Handbook of Counseling Psychology*, edited by Steven D. Brown and Robert W. Lent. New York: Wiley, pp. 383–416.

Gilmore, David. 2009. *Monsters: Evil Beings, Mythical Beasts and All Manner of Imaginary Terrors*. Philadelphia: University of Pennsylvania Press.

Global Fund for Women. n.d. "Measuring a year in global resistance and interconnected movements." https://www.globalfundforwomen.org/year-in-resistance-womens-march.

Gorham, Deborah. 1978. "'The maiden tribute of modern Babylon' re-examined: Child prostitution and the idea of childhood in late-Victorian England." *Victorian Studies* 21(3): 353–79.

Gorman, Stacy, Elizabeth Monk-Turner, and Jennifer N. Fish. 2010. "Free adult Internet web sites: How prevalent are degrading acts?" *Gender Issues* 27(3–4): 131–45.

Grady, Constance. 2020. "Some say the MeToo movement has gone too far: The Harvey Weinstein verdict proves that's false." *Vox*, February 24. https://www.vox.com/culture/2020/2/24/21150966/harvey-weinstein-rape-conviction-sexual-predatory-assault-me-too-too-far.

Griffin, Susan. 1971. "Rape: The all-American crime." *Ramparts* 10(3): 26–35.

Gross, Terry. 2019a. "Ronan Farrow: 'Catch and kill' tactics protected both Weinstein and Trump." *Fresh Air*. National Public Radio, Podcast audio, October 15. https://www.npr.org/2019/10/15/770249717/ronan-farrow-catch-and-kill-tactics-protected-both-weinstein-and-trump.

Gross, Terry. 2019b. "'She said' reveals the people and practices that protected Weinstein." *Fresh Air*. National Public Radio, Podcast audio, September 10. https://www.npr.org/transcripts/759384251?storyId=759384251.

Grosz, Elizabeth. 1994. *Volatile Bodies: Toward a Corporeal Feminism*. Bloomington: Indiana University Press.

Grove, Lloyd. 2020. "Why can't these ex-Fox News women get new TV jobs?" *Daily Beast*, January 24. https://www.thedailybeast.com/why-cant-these-ex-fox-news-women-get-new-tv-jobs.

Guadalupe-Diaz, Xavier. 2015. "Same-sex victimization and the LGBTQ community." In *Sexual Victimization: Then and Now*, edited by Tara N. Richards and Catherine D. Marcum. Thousand Oaks, CA: SAGE, pp. 173–92.

Hanson, Karl, R. Rocco Gizzarelli, and Heather Scott. 1994. "The attitudes of incest offenders: Sexual entitlement and acceptance of sex with children." *Criminal Justice and Behavior* 21(2): 187–202.

Haraway, Donna. 1991. *Simians, Cyborgs, and Women: The Reinvention of Nature*. New York: Routledge.

Harding, Kate. 2015. *Asking for It*. Boston, MA: DaCapo Press.

Harp, Dustin. 2018. "Misogyny in the 2016 US presidential election." In *Mediating Misogyny: Gender, Technology and Harassment*, edited by Jacqueline Vickery and Tracy Everbach. Cham: Palgrave Macmillan, pp. 189–207.

Harrell, Erika. 2017. "Crime against persons with disabilities, 2009–2015: Statistical tables." US Department of Justice, Office of Justice Programs, Bureau of Justice Statistics.

Harvard Business Review. 2019. "The #MeToo backlash." *Harvard Business Review*, September–October. https://hbr.org/2019/09/the-metoo-backlash.

Harvey, Paul and Martin J. Martinko. 2009. "An empirical examination of the role of attributions in psychological entitlement and its outcomes." *Journal of Organizational Behavior* 30: 459–76.

Hassan, Naeemul, Manash Kumar Mandal, Mansurul Bhuiyan, Aparna Moitra, and Syed Ishtiaque Ahmed. 2019. "Nonparticipation of Bangladeshi women in #Metoo movement." In *Proceedings of the Tenth International Conference on Information and Communication Technologies and Development*. New York: ACM, pp. 1–5. doi: 10.1145/3287098.3287125.

Hayek, Salma. 2017. "Harvey Weinstein is my monster too." *New York Times*, December 13. https://www.nytimes.com/interactive/2017/12/13/opinion/contributors/salma-hayek-harvey-weinstein.html.

Hayes, Dade and Dawn C. Chmielewski. 2018. "Harvey Weinstein's salary, perks, and code of conduct: Read his employment contract." *Deadline*, June 7. https://deadline.com/2018/06/harvey-weinstein-salary-perks-code-of-conduct-employment-contract-1202405670.

Haywood, Holly and Eric Swank. 2008. "Rape myths among Appalachian college students." *Violence and Victims* 23(3): 373–89.

Herman, Dianne. 1984. "The rape culture." In *Women: A Feminist Perspective*, edited by Jo Freeman. Mountain View, CA: Mayfield, pp. 45–53.

Hill, Melanie S. and Ann R. Fischer. 2001. "Does entitlement mediate the link between masculinity and rape-related variables?" *Journal of Counseling Psychology* 48(1): 39–50.

Hsu, V. Jo. 2019. "(Trans) forming #MeToo: Toward a networked response to gender violence." *Women's Studies in Communication* 42(3): 269–86.

Human Rights Campaign and Trans People of Color Coalition. 2017. *A Time to Act: Fatal Violence against Transgender People in America*. Washington,

DC. http://assets2.hrc.org/files/assets/resources/A_Time_To_Act_2017_REV3.pdf.

Human Rights Watch. 2012. *Cultivating Fear: The Vulnerability of Immigrant Farmworkers in the US to Sexual Violence and Sexual Harassment.* May 15. https://www.hrw.org/report/2012/05/15/cultivating-fear/vulnerability-immigrant-farmworkers-us-sexual-violence-and-sexual.

INCITE! n.d. Resources for Organizing. Subdirectory. https://incite-national.org/community-accountability.

Jacobs, Shayna. 2020. "Harvey Weinstein guilty on two charges, acquitted on others in New York sexual assault case." *Washington Post*, February 24. https://www.washingtonpost.com/lifestyle/harvey-weinstein-trial-verdict/2020/02/24/057b9f36-5284-11ea-b119-4faabac6674f_story.html.

Jacobs, Tom. 2019. "Black women are more likely than white women to report sexual harassment." *Pacific Standard*, June 24. https://psmag.com/news/black-women-are-more-likely-than-white-women-to-report-sexual-harassment.

Jacquet, Catherine O. 2019. *The Injustices of Rape.* Chapel Hill: University of North Carolina Press.

Jane, Emma A. 2014. "Your a ugly, whorish, slut: Understanding e-bile." *Feminist Media Studies* 14(4): 531–46.

Johnson, Stephanie K., Ksenia Keplinger, Jessica F. Kirk, and Liza Barnes. 2019. "Has sexual harassment at work decreased since #MeToo?" *Harvard Business Review*, July 18. https://hbr.org/2019/07/has-sexual-harassment-at-work-decreased-since-metoo?referral=03759&cm_vc=rr_item_page.bottom.

Jones, Graham M. 2014. "Secrecy." *Annual Review of Anthropology* 43: 53–69.

Kaminer, Wendy. 2018. "The dangers of vigilante feminism." *Spiked Online*, January 29. https://www.spiked-online.com/2018/01/29/the-dangers-of-vigilante-feminism.

Kantor, Jodi and Meg Twohey. 2017. "Harvey Weinstein paid off sexual harassment accusers for decades." *New York Times*, October 5.

Katz, Jackson. 2006. *The Macho Paradox: Why Some Men Hurt Women and How All Men Can Help*. Naperville, IL: SourceBooks.

Keller, Jessalynn, Kaitlynn Mendes, and Jessica Ringrose. 2018. "Speaking 'unspeakable things': Documenting digital feminist responses to rape culture." *Journal of Gender Studies* 27(1): 22–36.

Kellner, Douglas M. 1995. *Media Culture: Cultural Studies, Identity and Politics between the Modern and the Postmodern*. New York: Routledge.

Kelly, Liz. 1988. *Surviving Sexual Violence*. Minneapolis: University of Minnesota Press.

Kersten, Katherine. 2019. "False feminism: How we got from sexual liberation to #MeToo." January 28. https://www.americanexperiment.org/2019/01/false-feminism-got-sexual-liberation-metoo.

Kimmel, Michael. 2005. *The Gender of Desire*. Buffalo, NY: SUNY Press.

Kingston, Anne. 2014. "How Jian Ghomeshi got away with it." *Macleans*, November 6. https://www.macleans.ca/news/canada/jian-ghomeshi-how-he-got-away-with-it.

Kirby, Jen. 2018a. "Bill Cosby paid accuser Andrea Constand nearly $3.4 million in a 2006 settlement." *Vox*, April 9. https://www.vox.com/2018/4/9/17217210/bill-cosby-retrial-andrea-constand-settlement-3-4-million-retrial.

Kirby, Jen. 2018b. "The sexual abuse scandal surrounding USA gymnastics team doctor Larry Nassar, explained." *Vox*, May 6. https://www.vox.com/identities/2018/1/19/16897722/sexual-abuse-usa-gymnastics-larry-nassar-explained.

Kitroeff, Natalie. 2020. "Mexico's president claims 90% of domestic violence calls are 'false.'" *New York Times*, May 31.

Larabee, Ann. 2017. "Pussy hats as social movement symbols." *Journal of Popular Culture* 50(2): 215–17.

Larson, Sarah. 2015. "Spotlight and its revelations." *New Yorker*, December 8. https://www.newyorker.com/culture/sarah-larson/spotlight-and-its-revelations.

Lauzen, Martha M. 2018. *The Celluloid Ceiling: Behind-the-Scenes Employment of Women on the Top 100, 250 and 500 Films of 2018*. San Diego, CA: Center for the Study of Women in Film and Television. https://womenintvfilm.sdsu.edu/wp-content/uploads/2019/01/2018_Celluloid_Ceiling_Report.pdf.

Letourneau, Charles. 1891. *The Evolution of Marriage and the Family*. London: Walter Scott.

Levine, John and Itay Hod. 2017. "What did NBC know about Matt Lauer and when?" *The Wrap*, December 1. https://www.thewrap.com/matt-lauer-sexual-what-did-nbc-know-today.

Lilla, Mark. 2016. "The end of identity liberalism." Sunday Review. *New York Times*, November 18. https://www.nytimes.com/2016/11/20/opinion/sunday/the-end-of-identity-liberalism.html?_r=0.

Lin, Zhongxuan and Liu Yang. 2019. "Individual and collective empowerment: Women's voices in the #MeToo movement in China." *Asian Journal of Women's Studies* 25(1): 117–31.

Lind, Dara. 2016. "Poll: Vast majority of Trump voters don't care much about the leaked Trump tape." *Vox*, October 9. https://www.vox.com/2016/10/9/13217158/polls-donald-trump-assault-tape.

Linskey, Annie and Sean Sullivan. 2020. "Allegation against Biden prompts reexamination of 'Believe Women.'" *Washington Post*, May 3. https://www.washingtonpost.com/politics/allegation-against-biden-prompts-reexamination-of-believe-women/2020/05/02/00741eb0-8a5a-11ea-9dfd-990f9dcc71fc_story.html.

Lonsway, Kimberly A. and Louise F. Fitzgerald. 1994. "Rape myths: In review." *Psychology of Women Quarterly* 18(2): 133–64.

Lowe, Michelle and Paul Rogers. 2017. "The scope of male rape: A selective review of research, policy and practice." *Aggression and Violent Behavior* 35: 38–43.

Lucero, Gabrielle. 2015. "Military sexual assault: Reporting and rape culture." *Sanford Journal of Public Policy* 6(1): 1–32.

MacGillivray, Emily J. 2016. "Women's and feminist activism in the Native United States and Canada." In *The Wiley Blackwell Encyclopedia of Gender and Sexuality Studies*, edited by Nancy A. Naples. Malden, MA: John Wiley & Sons, pp. 1–5.

MacKinnon, Catharine A. 1979. *Sexual Harassment of Working Women: A Case of Sex Discrimination.* New Haven, CT: Yale University Press.

MacKinnon, Catharine A. 2016. “Rape redefined.” *Harvard Law and Policy Review* 10: 431–77.

Mallenbaum, Carly, Paul Ryan, and Maria Puente. 2018. “A complete list of the 60 Bill Cosby accusers and their reaction to his prison sentence.” *People*, September 26. https://www.usatoday.com/story/life/people/2018/04/27/bill-cosby-full-list-accusers/555144002.

Mallory, Christy, Amira Hasenbush, and Brad Sears. 2015. “Discrimination and harassment by law enforcement officers in the LGBT community.” The Williams Institute at UCLA, Los Angeles. https://escholarship.org/content/qt5663q0w1/qt5663q0w1.pdf.

Malone, Carolyn. 1999. “Sensational stories, endangered bodies: Women's work and the new journalism in England in the 1890s.” *Albion* 31(1): 49–71.

Malone, Noreen. 2015. “I'm no longer afraid: 35 women tell their stories about being assaulted by Bill Cosby, and the culture that wouldn't listen.” *New York Magazine: The Cut*, July 26. https://www.thecut.com/2015/07/bill-cosbys-accusers-speak-out.html.

Mao, Frances. 2019. “2019 election: Why politics is toxic for Australian women.” BBC News, May 16. https://www.bbc.com/news/world-australia-48197145.

Mardorossian, Carine. 2014. *Framing the Rape Victim: Gender and Agency Reconsidered*. New Brunswick, NJ: Rutgers University Press.

Marotta, Jenna. 2018. “#MeToo founder Tarana Burke: Movement is ‘not about taking down powerful men.’” *IndieWire*, May 31. https://www.indiewire.com/2018/05/tarana-burke-me-too-daily-show-trevor-noah-interview-1201969962.

Martin, Nick. 2019. "The connection between pipelines and sexual violence." *New Republic*, October 15.

Matthews, Nancy. 2005. *Confronting Rape: The Feminist Anti-Rape Movement and the State*. New York: Routledge.

McGowan, Rose. 2018. *Brave*. New York: HarperOne.

McGuire, Danielle L. 2010. *At the Dark End of the Street: Black Women, Rape, and Resistance: A New History of the Civil Rights Movement from Rosa Parks to the Rise of Black Power.* New York: Vintage.

McKinney, Debra. 2006. "Reporting on rape trauma." In *Covering Violence*, edited by Roger Simpson and William Edward Coté. New York: Columbia University Press, pp. 201–21.

Mehmood, Rabia. 2018. "Pakistan's long #MeToo moment." Al Jazeera, April 22. https://www.aljazeera.com/indepth/opinion/pakistan-long-metoo-moment-180422151525450.html.

Mendes, Kaitlynn, Jessica Ringrose, and Jessalynn Keller. 2018. "MeToo and the promise and pitfalls of challenging rape culture through digital feminist activism." *European Journal of Women's Studies* 25(2): 236–46.

Meyers, Marian. 1997. *News Coverage of Violence against Women: Engendering Blame*. Thousand Oaks, CA: SAGE.

Miami Herald and McClatchy Newspapers. 2019. "Perversion of justice." December 19. https://www.youtube.com/watch?v=-u7_j6CWbCU&list=PLW6BLXAZb_to0b_PiaM6XoFY4K_jbW1MF.

Monitor. 2014. "Desire Luzinda should be locked up and isolated." November 4.

Morgan, Rachel E. and Barbara A. Oudekerk. 2018.

"Criminal Victimization, 2018." US Department of Justice, Bureau of Justice Statistics, Washington, DC. https://www.bjs.gov/content/pub/pdf/cv18.pdf.

Mundy, Liza. 2012. "Foxy ladies." *The Atlantic*, September. https://www.theatlantic.com/magazine/archive/2012/09/foxy-ladies/309054.

Murray, Melissa V. 2017. "We won't let *TIME* erase Tarana Burke from the movement she started." BET, December 7, 2017.

Musto, Jennifer. 2019. "Transing critical criminology: A critical unsettling and transformative anti-carceral feminist reframing." *Critical Criminology* 27(1): 37–54.

Naff, Lycia. 2014. "Exclusive: Bill Cosby threw me down on his bed and pinned me by the neck." *DailyMailOnline*, October 27. https://www.dailymail.co.uk/news/article-2806437/Bill-Cosby-threw-bed-pinned-neck-ll-never-forget-sound-clinking-belt-buckle-Actress-lifts-lid-harrowing-years-rape-hands-TV-legend.html.

National Sexual Violence Resource Center. 2012. "False reporting." Washington, DC: US Department of Justice, Office on Violence against Women. https://www.nsvrc.org/sites/default/files/Publications_NSVRC_Overview_False-Reporting.pdf.

Nava, Mica. 1988. "Cleveland and the press: Outrage and anxiety in the reporting of child sexual abuse." *Feminist Review* 28: 103–21.

NBC News. 2018. "Women in media report highest rates of sexual harassment among white-collar industries." July 25. https://www.nbcnews.com/news/us-news/women-media-reported-highest-rates-sexual-harassment-among-white-collar-n894626.

New York Daily Times. 1851. "Woman's Rights." October 18.

North, Anna. 2019. "The connections between Donald Trump, Harvey Weinstein, and the *National Enquirer*, explained." *Vox*, October 22. https://www.vox.com/identities/2019/10/22/20920810/trump-harvey-weinstein-national-enquirer-ami-allegations.

North, Anna. 2020. "The women's marches are shrinking: Their influence isn't." *Vox*, January 17. https://www.vox.com/2020/1/17/21068870/2020-womens-march-washington-election-women-voting.

Nurik, Chloé. 2018. "50 shades of film censorship: Gender bias from the Hays Code to MPAA ratings." *Communication Culture & Critique* 11(4): 530–47.

Nyong'o, Lupita. 2017. "Lupita Nyong'o: Speaking out about Harvey Weinstein." *New York Times*, October 19. https://www.nytimes.com/2017/10/19/opinion/lupita-nyongo-harvey-weinstein.html.

Office for Victims of Crime. 2014. *Responding to Transgender Victims of Sexual Assault*. June. https://www.ovc.gov/pubs/forge/sexual_numbers.html.

Ohlheiser, Abby. 2018. "How #MeToo really was different, according to the data." *Washington Post*, January 22. https://www.washingtonpost.com/news/the-intersect/wp/2018/01/22/how-metoo-really-was-different-according-to-data.

Onwuachi-Willig, Angela. 2018. "What about #UsToo: The invisibility of race in the #MeToo movement." *Yale Law Journal* 128: 105–20.

Osipova, Natalia V. and Chloe Melas. 2020. "How one of Harvey Weinstein's first accusers is fighting back and empowering others." CNN, March 9. https://

www.cnn.com/2020/03/09/entertainment/ambra-gutierrez-model-alliance/index.html.

Paiva, Raquel. 2019. "#MeToo, feminism and femicide in Brazil." *Interactions: Studies in Communication & Culture* 10(3): 241–55.

Palazzolo, Joe, Michael Rothfeld, and Lukas Alpert. 2016. "*National Enquirer* shielded Donald Trump from *Playboy* model's affair allegation." *Wall Street Journal*, November 4. https://www.wsj.com/articles/national-enquirer-shielded-donald-trump-from-playboy-models-affair-allegation-1478309380.

Paulins, V. Ann, Julie L. Hillery, Alexandra L. Howell, and Nancy L. Malcom. 2017. "Exploring the meaning of the Pussyhat." *International Textile and Apparel Association (ITAA) Annual Conference Proceedings*. https://lib.dr.iastate.edu/itaa_proceedings/2017/presentations/74.

Perloff, Richard M. 2000. "The press and lynchings of African Americans." *Journal of Black Studies* 30(3): 315–30.

Pew Research Center. 2017. "Online harassment." https://www.pewresearch.org/internet/2017/07/11/online-harassment-2017.

Phillips, Nickie D. 2017. *Beyond Blurred Lines: Rape Culture in Popular Media*. Lanham, MD: Rowman & Littlefield.

Phipps, Alison. 2019. "The political whiteness of #MeToo." Red Pepper, June 4. https://www.redpepper.org.uk/the-political-whiteness-of-metoo.

Pilon, Mary. 2019. "How much are little girls worth?" *Fortune*, July.

Pollitt, Katha. 1995. *Reasonable Creatures*. New York: Vintage.

Prasad, Vasundhara. 2018. "If anyone is listening, #Metoo: Breaking the culture of silence around sexual abuse through regulating non-disclosure agreements and secret settlements." *Boston College Law Review* 59(7): 2507–49.

The Pussyhat Project. 2020. Design interventions for social change. Website. https://www.pussyhatproject.com/our-story.

Radu, Sintia. 2017. "How #MeToo has awoken women around the world." *US News & World Report*, October 25. https://www.usnews.com/news/best-countries/articles/2017-10-25/how-metoo-has-awoken-women-around-the-world.

Rashid, Tahmina. 2019. "#MeToo: A mixed response from Pakistan." *Policy Forum*. Canberra, Australia: Asia & The Pacific Policy Society. December. https://www.policyforum.net/metoo-a-mixed-response-from-pakistan.

Reilly, Katie. 2019. "What revived the case against Jeffrey Epstein." *TIME*, July 22.

Rentschler, Carrie A. 2017. "Bystander intervention, feminist hashtag activism, and the anti-carceral politics of care." *Feminist Media Studies* 17(4): 565–84.

Rezack, Sherene. 1998. *Looking White People in the Eye: Gender, Race and Culture in Courtroom and Classrooms*. Toronto: University of Toronto Press.

Rodino-Colocino, Michelle. 2018. "Me too, #MeToo: Countering cruelty with empathy." *Communication and Critical/Cultural Studies* 15(1): 96–100.

Rooted in Rights. 2018. "Video: #Disability Too." May 24. https://rootedinrights.org/video/disabilitytoo.

Rosenblatt, Valerie. 2012. "Hierarchies, power

inequalities, and organizational corruption." *Journal of Business Ethics* 111(2): 237–51.

Ross-Pilkington, Jack. 2017. "Mass incarceration and police violence in Native American communities." November 3. Ithaca, NY: Cornell University. https://www.cornellrooseveltinstitute.org/dom/mass-incarceration-and-police-violence-in-native-american-communities.

Roth, Kenneth. 2017. "The dangerous rise of populism: Global attacks on human rights values." *Journal of International Affairs* 70 (anniversary issue): 79–84.

Russo, Ann. 2001. *Taking Back Our Lives: A Call to Action for the Feminist Movement*. New York: Routledge.

Ryan, Kathryn M. 2011. "The relationship between rape myths and sexual scripts: The social construction of rape." *Sex Roles* 65(11/12): 774–82.

Sanders, Mia. 2018. "#MeToo: The personal is still political." *Green Left Weekly* 1166.

Saner, Emine. 2013. "Top 10 sexist moments in politics: Julia Gillard, Hillary Clinton, and more." *Guardian*, June 14. https://www.theguardian.com/politics/2013/jun/14/top-10-sexist-moments-politics.

Savage, Mark. 2019. "R. Kelly: The history of allegations against him." BBC News, August 6. https://www.bbc.com/news/entertainment-arts-40635526.

Scaptura, Maria N. and Kaitlin M. Boyle. 2020. "Masculinity threat, 'incel' traits, and violent fantasies among heterosexual men in the United States." *Feminist Criminology* 15(3): 278–98.

Scherer, Heidi and Bradford W. Reyns. 2019. "Visible disabilities and risk of interpersonal victimization." In

Appearance Bias and Crime, edited by Bonnie Berry. New York: Cambridge University Press, pp. 243–54.

Schmidt, Grace Speights, Margaret E. Rodgers, and Jocelyn R. Cuttino to Special Committee of the NPR Board of Directors. 2018. "Report of independent investigation into allegations of sexual harassment at NPR." Morgan Lewis, February 19.

Schoenfeld, Heather. 2018. *Building the Prison State: Race and the Politics of Mass Incarceration*. Chicago, IL: University of Chicago Press.

Schwartz, Shalom H., Gian Vittorio Caprara, and Michele Vecchione. 2010. "Basic personal values, core political values, and voting: A longitudinal analysis." *Political Psychology* 31(3): 421–52.

Searles, Patricia and Ronald J. Berger. 1995. "Feminist foundations for the study of rape and society." In *Rape and Society: Readings on the Problem of Sexual Assault*, edited by Patricia Searles and Ronald J. Berger. Boulder, CO: Westview Press, pp. 1–6.

Shapiro, Joseph. 2018. "How prosecutors changed the odds to start winning some of the toughest rape cases." *All Things Considered*. National Public Radio, January 16. https://www.npr.org/2018/01/16/577063976/its-an-easy-crime-to-get-away-with-but-prosecutors-are-trying-to-change-that.

Sherman, Gabriel. 2016. "Former Fox News booker says she was sexually harassed and 'psychologically tortured' by Roger Ailes for more than 20 years." *New York Magazine: The Daily Intelligencer*, July 29. https://nymag.com/intelligencer/2016/07/fmr-fox-booker-harassed-by-ailes-for-20-years.html.

Smith, Sarah Francis and Scott O. Lilienfeld. 2013. "Psychopathy in the workplace: The knowns and unknowns." *Aggression and Violent Behavior* 18: 2014–18.

Smith, Sharon G., Jieru Chen, Kathleen C. Basile, Leah K. Gilbert, Melissa T. Merrick, Nimesh Patel, Margi Walling, and Anurag Jain. 2017. *The National Intimate Partner and Sexual Violence Survey (NISVS): 2010–2012 State Report.* Atlanta, GA: National Center for Injury Prevention and Control, Centers for Disease Control and Prevention.

Snider, Mike. 2017. "Fox's bill for Roger Ailes settlements is now $45 million." *USA Today*, May 10. https://www.usatoday.com/story/money/business/2017/05/10/foxs-bill-roger-ailes-settlements-now-45-million/101515930.

Snow, Jason N., Roy M. Kern, and William L. Curlette. 2001. "Identifying personality traits associated with attrition in systematic training for effective parenting groups." *Family Journal: Counseling and Therapy for Couples and Families* 9(2): 102–8.

Soderlund, Gretchen. 2002. "Covering urban vice: *The New York Times*, 'white slavery,' and the construction of journalistic knowledge." *Critical Studies in Media Communication* 19(4): 438–60.

Spohn, Cassia and Katharine Tellis. 2012. "The criminal justice system's response to sexual violence." *Violence Against Women* 18(2): 169–92.

Stacey, Michele, Kimberly H. Martin, and Bradley T. Brick. 2017. "Victim and suspect race and the police clearance of sexual assault." *Race and Justice* 7(3): 226–55.

Stanglin, Doug. 2017. "Report: Fox kept Bill O'Reilly despite $32m sexual harassment settlement." *USA Today*, October 21. https://www.usatoday.

com/story/news/2017/10/21/report-bill-oreilly-struck-sexual-harassment-deal-january-former-fox-analyst/787360001.

Stanko, Elizabeth. 1990. *Everyday Violence: How Men and Women Experience Sexual and Physical Danger*. London: Pandora.

Stein, Mark. 2012. *Rethinking the Gay and Lesbian Movement*. New York: Routledge.

Stockman, Farah. 2018. "One year after women's march, more activism but less unity." *New York Times*, January 15. https://www.nytimes.com/2018/01/15/us/womens-march-anniversary.html.

Stockton, Will. 2017. "Discourse and the history of sexuality." In *Clinical Encounters in Sexuality: Psychoanalysis and Queer Theory*, edited by Noreen Giffney and Eve Watson. Goleta, CA: Punctum Books, pp. 171–94.

Stoltenberg, John. 1989. *Refusing to Be a Man: Essays on Sex and Justice*. New York: Meridian.

Stone, Meighan and Rachel Vogelstein. 2019. "Celebrating #MeToo's global impact." *Foreign Policy*, March 7.

Stotzer, Rebecca L. 2009. "Violence against transgender people: A review of United States data." *Aggression and Violent Behavior* 14(3): 170–9.

Stuart, Shauna. 2019. "How Tarana Burke founded 'Me, Too' movement in Selma, Alabama." AP (Associated Press) News, January 18. https://apnews.com/12e86aa615484aa8b8d1a1d4fa45e584.

Swaine, John. 2018. "*National Enquirer* owner admits to 'catch and kill' payment to ex-playmate." *Guardian*, December 12. https://www.theguardian.com/us-news/

2018/dec/12/national-enquirer-trump-payments-david-pecker-catch-and-kill.

Taylor, Chloë. 2018. "Anti-carceral feminism and sexual assault—a defense: A critique of the critique of the critique of carceral feminism." *Social Philosophy Today* 34: 29–49.

Taylor, Chloë. 2019. *Foucault, Feminism and Sex Crimes: An Anti-Carceral Analysis*. New York: Routledge.

Taylor, Rae. 2009. "Slain and slandered: A content analysis of the portrayal of femicide in crime news." *Homicide Studies* 13(1): 21–49.

Taylor, Verta and Leila J. Rupp. 1993. "Women's culture and lesbian feminist activism: A reconsideration of cultural feminism." *Signs: Journal of Women in Culture and Society* 19(1): 32–61.

Terkel, Amanda. 2016. "Woman who worked at Fox News says she had to wear her 'skirts short' and her 'heels high.'" *Huffington Post*, July 8. https://www.huffpost.com/entry/diane-dimond-fox-news_n_577f0095e4b0344d514eb1d5.

Thenappan, Bala. 2020. "Interview with the *Boston Globe*'s Walter Robinson." *Penn Political Review*, February 1. https://pennpoliticalreview.org/2020/02/interview-with-the-boston-globes-walter-robinson.

Tillman, Shaquita, Thelma Bryant-Davis, Kimberly Smith, and Alison Marks. 2010. "Shattering silence: Exploring barriers to disclosure for African American sexual assault survivors." *Trauma, Violence, & Abuse* 11(2): 59–70.

TIME. 2019. "Our pain is never prioritized." *TIME*, April 23. https://time.com/5574163/tarana-burke-metoo-time-100-summit.

Time's Up. 2020. "Our Story." https://timesupnow.org/about/our-story.

Todorov, Tzvetan. 1999. *The Conquest of America: The Question of the Other*. Norman: University of Oklahoma Press.

Trombino, Caryn and Markus Funk. 2019. *Report of the Independent Investigation: Sexual Abuse Committed by Dr. Richard Strauss at the Ohio State University*. May 15. https://compliance.osu.edu/assets/site/pdf/Revised_report.pdf.

Trotter, J. K. 2013. "Fox News uses a 'leg cam' to ogle female panelists." Gawker, November 22. https://gawker.com/fox-news-uses-a-leg-cam-to-ogle-female-panelists-legs-1469841162.

Truman, Dana M., David M. Tokar, and Ann R. Fischer. 1996. "Dimensions of masculinity: Relations to date rape supportive attitudes and sexual aggression in dating situations." *Journal of Counseling & Development* 74(6): 555–62.

Uggens, Christopher and Amy Blackston. 2004. "Sexual harassment as a gendered expression of power." *American Sociological Review* 3: 64–92.

United Nations. 2006. *Ending Violence against Women: From Words to Action*. https://www.unwomen.org/-/media/headquarters/media/publications/un/en/englishstudy.pdf?la=en&vs=954.

Uribe, Raquel Coronelle and Sixiao Yu. 2020. "#MeToo founder Tarana Burke reflects on movement at Institute of Politics." *Harvard Crimson*, February 27. https://www.thecrimson.com/article/2020/2/27/tarana-burke-iop-metoo.

Usborne, David. 2018. "The peacock patriarchy." *Esquire*, September 1.

Utt, Jamie. 2014. "Stop thinking like a perpetrator: 4 ways to better support survivors of sexual violence." *Everyday Feminism*, September 2. https://everydayfeminism.com/2014/09/stop-thinking-like-a-perpetrator.

Valenti, Jessica. 2013. "How to write about rape: Rules for journalists." *The Nation*, October 25. https://www.thenation.com/article/archive/how-write-about-rape-rules-journalists.

Vitis, Laura and Fairleigh Gilmour. 2016. "Dick pics on blast: A woman's resistance to online sexual harassment using humour, art and Instagram." *Crime, Media, Culture* 13(3): 335–55.

Walker, Alice. 2011. "Advancing Luna—and Ida B. Wells." In Alice Walker, *You Can't Keep a Good Woman Down: Stories*. New York: Open Road, pp. 85–104.

Ward, Monique L., Ann Merriwether, and Allison Caruthers. 2006. "Breasts are for men: Media, masculinity ideologies, and men's beliefs about women's bodies." *Sex Roles* 55(9–10): 703–14.

Way, Katie. 2018. "I went on a date with Aziz Ansari: It turned into the worst night of my life." Babe.net, January 13. https://babe.net/2018/01/13/aziz-ansari-28355.

Weaver, Gina Marie. 2012. *Ideologies of Forgetting: Rape in the Vietnam War*. Albany, NY: SUNY Press.

Weaver, Hilary N. 2009. "The colonial context of violence: Reflections on violence in the lives of Native American women." *Journal of Interpersonal Violence* 24(9): 1552–63.

Wolf, Naomi. 1991. *The Beauty Myth: How Images of Beauty Are Used Against Women*. New York: Anchor.

Woodhull, Winifred. 1988. "Sexuality, power, and the question of rape." In *Feminism and Foucault: Reflections on Resistance*, edited by Irene Diamond and Lee Quimby. Boston, MA: Northeastern University Press, pp. 167–76.

World Health Organization. 2012. "Sexual violence." https://apps.who.int/iris/bitstream/handle/10665/77434/WHO_RHR_12.37_eng.pdf;jsessionid=3E2D08AB67F02A8F34301A014DD37E32?sequence=1.

Wykes, Maggie. 1998. "A family affair: The British press, sex, and the Wests." In *News, Gender, and Power*, edited by Cynthia Carter, Gill Branston, and Stuart Allen. New York: Routledge, pp. 133–47.

Yung, Judy. 1995. *Unbound Feet: A Social History of Chinese Women in San Francisco*. Berkeley: University of California Press.

Zacharek, Stephanie, Eliana Dockterman, and Haley Sweetland Edwards. 2017. "2017 Person of the Year: The Silence Breakers." *TIME*, December 18.

Zadnik, Liz and Enid Melendez. 2014. *Fact Sheet: Sexual Violence and the Impact on Latin@ Communities*. Enola: Pennsylvania Coalition Against Rape.

Zamalin, Alex. 2017. *Struggle on Their Minds: The Political Thought of African American Resistance*. New York: Columbia University Press.

Index

Index

Index